FROM MY
BAKERY PERCH

FROM MY

BAKERY PERCH

Memories of growing up in Boston's "Little Italy"
1927–1958

With

RECIPES FROM THE HOMELAND
A collection of Italian Family Recipes

Vita Orlando Sinopoli

Charter Street Press
P.O. Box 906
Wilmington, MA 01887

To order additional copies of this book, contact:
Xlibris Corporation
1-888-795-4274
www.Xlibris.com
Orders@Xlibris.com
16704

CONTENTS

PART ONE

FROM MY BAKERY PERCH

PART TWO

RECIPES FROM THE HOMELAND

Festive Cookies and Pastries

Dedicated to the memory of my parents

Pietro and Lucia (LaGrassa) Orlando

and my brother

Peter A. Orlando, Jr.

ACKNOWLEDGMENTS

Without the encouragement and patience of my loving husband William, I could not have completed this project.

Genuine thanks to Joseph Marcantonio, DMD, for originally requesting that I write about having grown up in Boston's North End. My thanks to Pamela Donnaruma, Editor, *Post-Gazette*, Boston, MA for publishing my articles and all my recipes.

Heartfelt thanks to my daughter Donna Meuse, who worked tirelessly in organizing this book for publication. Sincere thanks also to my daughter Vita Marie Graham, my son Bill Sinopoli and granddaughter Kristina Meuse for proofreading and selecting photographs. My thanks to Phyllis Kelly and Rita Pinto for their guidance and encouragement. Special thanks to Marion Vuilleumier for her editing and for sharing her expertise in this field. I am very grateful to the members of the Twelve O'clock Scholars writing group, and also to members of Marion's writing workshop on Cape Cod for their critiquing and support. Thanks to the many relatives and friends who lent a hand by reminding me of events during our childhood, many of which I write about in this book.

PROLOGUE

The Boston waterfront was a pivotal force in creating the character of "North Boston," as it was known in colonial days. The North End of Boston had not always been an Italian community.

Early in the 1700s, Boston became an important seaport. Paul Revere, his father, and John Hancock, among others, operated successful businesses on the waterfront. Trade ships moved supplies in and out of the wharves that jutted into Boston Harbor. The wharves along the waterfront of Boston had numerous basket, leather, silver, spice and houseware shops where people purchased their needed items.

The seamen's Bethal and boarding houses in the North End of Boston housed Captains and their seamen waiting for new assignments. They frequented the taverns and coffee shops along the wharves as well as those on Ship and Ann Streets. These roads formed the perimeter of North Boston.

Passenger ships in the 1700s transported people along the coastal ports as far south as Virginia. They later traveled to Nova Scotia, New York and Provincetown, MA. Ocean vessels carried passengers to and from European countries. People boarding or embarking from these vessels visited the merchants on the waterfront and in North Boston. They strolled through the streets along with Samuel Adams, John Adams, John Hancock and even Benjamin Franklin, unaware of the Sons of Liberty and their plans for the new colony.

Immigrants arriving from various countries who planned to stay in Boston walked to the North End of Boston to find living quarters. Some boarded with relatives or friends until an apartment or rooms became available. The new arrivals received offerings of furniture and accessories from their new friends, neighbors and relatives. Because they chose to live near their own countrymen, this resulted in clusters of people from the same hometown living on the same street. Being near friends and relatives eased the anxiety of starting a new life in a strange environment. It took time to adjust to living near neighbors who came from different ethnic backgrounds and spoke a variety of languages.

Shifting tides of immigrants have changed the characteristics of the North End through the years. Families seeking freedom from oppression from Portugal, Spain, Russia, Greece, Syria and Armenia settled into Boston's North End during the early 1800s. The potato famines of Ireland brought Irish immigrants to Boston's shores around 1840. They began to replace the Greeks, Syrians, Chinese and Armenians who relocated their families to South Boston, while others settled in Cambridge and Somerville in the outskirts of Boston.

In the 1840s, the Irish established meat and grocery shops, taverns, and restaurants in the North End. They moved into the political arena during the 1880s. John "Honey Fitz" Fitzgerald (President John F. Kennedy's grandfather) lived on Garden Court Street in the North End. This is close to Paul Revere's house. "Honey Fitz" became a Representative and later Mayor of Boston. His daughter Rosemary Fitzgerald Kennedy (President Kennedy's mother) was born on Garden Court Street. While her father was Mayor, he moved his family to Auburn and then Dorchester. Other Irish families followed by also moving to outlying districts like Charlestown, Dorchester, Roxbury, and South Boston.

The Spanish, Portuguese and Italians began arriving at the shores of Boston around 1870. They developed lucrative fishing fleets along Commercial Street and Atlantic Avenue. This increased the activities in the City of Boston.

Crowded buildings, large families, and shortages of living quarters around 1890 in Boston's North End resulted in the removal of the smaller wooden homes of the community. Cold-water flats in three-or four-story red-brick buildings gradually replaced them. They lined the streets like sentinels standing side by side. In some areas, the buildings in the North End sprouted one behind the other, eliminating any space for family vegetable or flower gardens. Between the buildings there developed tiny courtyards, alleyways and narrow back streets. The dirt roads became cobblestone streets lined with narrow red-brick sidewalks.

During the late 1920s there lived a sprinkling of Irish, Spanish, and Portuguese families on North, Fleet, Hanover, and Battery Streets. Some Jewish and Greek families lived in the North Margin and Salem Street area close to the synagogues. The Chinese families moved into the South End where they established restaurants and a variety of Chinese food shops.

Prior to 1890, there were fewer than 5,000 Italian immigrants in Boston's North End. After World War I, the population in the small community (approximately the size of the Boston Common) increased to about 18,000 people. These residents had come from small villages and towns of Italy. They hoped to share the benefits of the Industrial Revolution. The population continued to increase until 1940.

Businesses owned by different ethnic groups continued to operate in the Blackstone Street, Faneuil Hall and Quincy market areas, and in the North End. Italians increased the number of taverns, restaurants, bakeries, produce, grocery, and meat markets in the community.

The bustling North End community during the Great Depression was filled with large and small low-income minority families. This community, often called "Little Italy," accommodated immigrants and their families, who dreamed, as my parents did, of earning a more comfortable existence in the New World.

PART ONE

FROM MY BAKERY PERCH

Memories of growing up in Boston's "Little Italy"
1927–1958

By

Vita Orlando Sinopoli

Charter Street Press

INTRODUCTION

Each busload of tourists visiting the Old North Church or Paul Revere's House in the North End of Boston was greeted by a group of children reciting "Paul Revere was married twice, had sixteen children, eleven boys and five girls."

I loved reciting the wonderful heritage of our tiny community. As children of Italian immigrants, we learned quickly the history of John Adams, John Hancock, Samuel Adams, Paul Revere, Joseph Warren and their longing to live in a free nation in the New World.

My introduction to the history of Boston began when my parents purchased a bakery on 41 Charter Street in 1927. I was three and my brother Peter was seven when we moved from Fitchburg, MA to Boston. We settled into a four-room, top-floor apartment on 38 Charter Street, a short distance from Copp's Hill Burying Ground. From my rear bedroom window, I could see the steeple top of the Old North Church located around the corner on Salem Street.

Peter and I loved living near grandparents, uncles, aunts, cousins and family friends whom my parents called "paesani"(friends from their homeland). Some of these people lived on the same street and others nearby. In this bilingual world, we spoke Italian in the presence of our parents and elders, but we spoke English in school and among our friends.

The bakery my parents owned, across the street from our apartment building, became our second home. The daily activities of the business that provided for our family through the depression years influenced our lives.

The memories in my book are experiences, as I remember them, while living in that compact Italian community from 1927 through 1958. I am happy to share these recollections with you.

Vita Orlando Sinopoli

Photo of Orlando Family

A BAKERY IN BOSTON'S NORTH END

The coals hissed and crackled as Mama lowered the new coals onto the hot, red embers in the potbellied stove. The heat from the small open door was soothing. The smell of the new coal filtered through the room and gave us additional heat. The welcomed heat from the potbellied stove added to the heat from the large white-tiled oven at the back of the workshop. Behind the potbellied stove stood a wooden half-wall that separated the workshop from the store. An oak ice chest with top sliding doors stood at the right of the potbellied stove. From the age of three, with the help of an empty wooden milk crate, I climbed onto the chest with my little pillow and surveyed the world around me. Looking into the workshop, I saw Papa and the assisting bakers. When I turned toward the store, I saw Mama gently organizing the fresh bread in the display window or greeting and serving customers. Whenever Mama had to get into the ice chest for a customer's milk or whenever Papa had to take out the one-pound blocks of yeast used in mixing the dough, I moved over. They slid open one of the doors and retrieved what they needed.

As I became older and attended school, I asked permission to spend time on my perch on top of the ice chest. I watched Mama dutifully sweeping floors and dusting shelves each day. She paused to converse with those who brought news from relatives in their homeland. Some came in the winter to spend time in the warmth of the bakery while others discussed problems with her or brought laughter into her day. Mama always had her knitting or crocheting with her and even her mending. She never wasted a moment.

I listened to a special concert created by the sounds around me. The bell attached to the top of the front door tingled as customers entered and exited. I heard the flow of water entering the mixer and the splish-splash of flour, yeast and sugar blending in its belly. The churning arms of the mixer growled loudly as they produced the necessary dough. Hugo, the baker in charge of the mixer, pressed the magic button at the proper time, causing the motor to hum. The mixer slowly rolled forward and down, bringing the opening face to face with Hugo. When he pushed another button, I heard the rasping sound of the dough breaker. Then the mixer stopped. He cut a portion of dough and guided it through the metal rollers of the dough breaker that seemed to cry out "I'm waiting, I'm waiting." He followed this procedure until the dough was the right consistency.

Papa stood with Turi, Toto, and "Tootsie" (Salvatore) at the large wooden trough table a few feet away. The chop-chop, clang-clang, of each piece of dough Papa handled added a rhythmic melody of its own as the dough danced from the table to scale and back until the piece was the correct weight.

These sounds were a signal to Mama to join Papa and the bakers at the bench. It didn't matter that the flour dust itched my eyes and made me sneeze. I enjoyed watching them roll out the one hundred or more loaves they prepared for baking. At times my eyes gave way to sleep, and I napped with my head resting on my folded arms on the partition.

Papa did not allow visitors into the workshop. Customers or visitors could only go as far as the opening in the store to the left of the potbellied stove. Perhaps that is why I enjoyed my "box seat" so much. I sat there even during quiet times and enjoyed the view of my two worlds.

Mama loved to roast chestnuts or cured black olives on the potbellied stove. "Go to Mr. Dorfman's store. Ask Harry to give you some black olives and Romano cheese," Mama said to my brother Peter. She paid for the items the next time she shopped.

Upon his return, Mama put the olives in a tin pie plate and placed the plate on the potbellied stove. We enjoyed our lunch of warm toasted olives, a piece of cheese, fresh bread and a drink of sarsaparilla or Moxie. We snacked on roasted chestnuts. I looked to see which customer took one before Mama offered.

When the gas odor from the coal became apparent in the bakery, I knew it was time for baking. The gas escaped from the oven as Toto lifted a ten-foot pole with a wet mop attached to it to clean the oven brick. The bakers did this before each baking. We heard hissing as water splashed onto the hot coals. More gas escaped from the oven. Watered-down bricks created steam for the bread to be baked.

One by one, with a twist of the wrist, Papa lifted the loaves off the cotton-lined breadbox. He placed the loaf onto a thin 8-inch-wide and 14-inch-long special board. With gentle ease, he slid six or seven loaves, one at a time, onto the wooden peel held by Toto. Toto opened the oven door with one hand. With two hands he guided the long ten-foot pole into the back of the oven. With a fast jerk and pull of the pole, the loaves slid onto the hot bricks in the oven. Another pull on the pole brought the peel and pole out of the oven. Toto closed the oven door. Papa, Hugo, Toto, and others mastered the art of slipping the loaves onto the hot bricks from the wooden peel.

As Toto maneuvered the bread and pole in and out of the oven, he entertained us with operatic arias or Italian melodies. He sang often while he worked. He not only entertained us, but also the tenants in the apartments above the bakery. His voice traveled with the aroma of the baking bread through the opened side door of the workshop, leading to the corridor entrance of the four-story building. The voice and aromas dispersed up the stairwell and into the above corridors.

Papa had three sets of bakers working eight-hour shifts. They baked bread for our retail and wholesale business. Seven trucks delivered to homes and businesses in the suburbs as far west as Framingham.

Days were long for all the family but especially for Papa. He waited for the truck drivers to return. Before retiring for the evening, he sat at his roll-top desk in the store and calculated the totals of each variety of bread listed on the worksheet completed by each driver. Papa computed his figures regarding quantity of ingredients and how many batches of bread the bakers needed to bake before six in the morning.

This routine caused us to often have our supper on a makeshift table in the workshop, away from any activities. We enjoyed supper more in our apartment without interruptions from customers or visitors. Even when we ate supper in the bakery, Papa always initiated family discussions that included our daily activities in school, our homework assignments, current news items or even politics during elections. The bakers meanwhile spaced their meal times around the work schedule, alternating so that production did not stop.

On Saturdays, when the last batch of bread came out of the oven, the bakers stacked the empty boxes on the four-wheel dollies. They moved them to one side of the workshop. Another baker swept the workshop. Someone else banked the oven, leaving it ready to start the coals the next afternoon.

I looked forward to leaving my perch on Saturday afternoons. People gathered throughout the day. The store remained open until ten in the evening or later, as did other merchants in the community.

Mama's sister and three brothers with their families lived close by. I anticipated the arrival of cousins or my friends MaryAnn or Jennie. I quickly asked if one or two children could join me in the workshop. Papa allowed me to do that on Saturday afternoons after the bakers finished their work.

We loved sitting on an empty dolly. We used our feet to glide on the dolly around the wooden workshop floor. We imagined being on a whirling amusement ride like those at Revere Beach.

When we got tired of that, we asked my parents to turn a breadbox over onto a few empty milk crates. It became our desk. We took pencils from Papa's desk and paper from the roll used to wrap bread. Mama gave us small scissors from her sewing basket. Aunt Lena and Mama taught us to fold paper and carefully cut curves and triangles into the folded pieces. The excitement intensified as we made our last cut into the paper. What is this creation going to look like, we asked ourselves. We prepared it to be a doily and anticipated seeing it as an edging on a shelf of our kitchen cupboard. It pleased us to see our artistic creation used together with those made by our parents.

The aroma of fresh-baked bread never impressed me as a child, perhaps because I was in its presence so much. However, as years pass, when I experience that aroma, it wells up a multitude of memories of the hundreds of people who touched our lives in Boston's "Little Italy" during the 1930s and '40s. Mostly I remember the number of hours I watched Mama and Papa work together tirelessly each day in their family business.

I REMEMBER LITTLE ITALY

In 1927, my parents, both immigrants from Italy, moved their family from Fitchburg, Massachusetts, to a little community along the northern waterfront of Boston. They had heard about the prospering Italian community of the North End. They purchased a small Italian bread bakery on Charter Street. We lived in a cold-water flat, across the street from the bakery, on the fourth floor of one of the red-brick tenements lining the street.

My brother Peter and I spent our time looking out the bakery windows, observing the passersby. The aroma of baking bread filled the air. Visitors came daily. Like my parents, merchants encouraged people to gather outside their stores or inside to chat. Customers stayed longer in the winter, soaking up the warmth from the hot ovens. Sometimes Mama allowed them to taste chestnuts roasting on top of the potbellied stove.

A walk down Salem and Cross Streets was like a tour through an obstacle course. For as far as you could see, crates and pushcarts lined the curbstones, filled with fruits and vegetables. Grocers added their barrels of olives, pickles, nuts, cheeses, tea and coffee beans. Houseware shops and hardware dealers displayed a variety of items outside and in their windows. On Fridays and Saturdays, people came from the suburbs to mingle with local shoppers on Blackstone Street and the adjoining market area packed with pushcart vendors.

In September and October, wine pressing became a family affair. Fathers purchased the grapes from freight cars in Charlestown. Family members gathered in the cellar of their apartment building. They diligently worked all day to squeeze the grapes for the wine that they stored in large wooden barrels. For several days our nostrils tingled with the smell of crushed grape skins. They spilled over onto the sidewalks from the boxes piled near each doorway. The aroma lasted even after the garbage collector removed them.

Aunt Anna spent time each day resting her elbows on the windowsill. She had trouble walking and avoided coming down from her third-floor apartment. When she saw the peddler of her choice, she called out to him or to one of us on the sidewalk. She placed the money for her purchase in a basket and lowered the basket tied to a rope. We paid for her items, and then saw to it that Aunt Anna's basket made a safe return.

Butchers knew how their customers wanted their meats cut. The grocer knew the products a customer preferred. Mama knew which loaf of bread the customer came in to purchase. She even knew which customers preferred sliced, whole, large or small loaves.

Like Mama, people checked out the prices of meats in the various markets by first looking at the window displays. The meats rested on layers of ice chips. During the Christmas and Easter holidays, the traditional meats used, like dressed lambs, rabbits and piglets, hung in the windows along with sides of beef, pork, and veal. Customers sometimes requested the butcher not to remove the fur from the rabbit. Some mothers planned to use it to trim a little girl's bonnet or coat collar after cleaning and drying the skin.

The aromas of the fruits and vegetables on Salem Street mingled with the smells from fish markets. We saw soaked, dried cod and haddock in tubs of water at Christmas time. We saw opened salted sardine and anchovy containers displayed near them. In season, I became fascinated by the snails making their way up the sides of the wooden barrel in front of the fish market.

On trips to the Commercial or Fulton Street chicken stores, I found the cackling annoying. The chickens cackled constantly as the clerk frequently opened the crate door. After taking out the chicken, he took it to be cleaned and dressed, unless the customer preferred to leave with a live chicken.

Pastry shops and bakeries prepared special Christmas and Easter delicacies during those holidays. Shoppers purchased some while others stopped to admire the colorful window displays.

In the summer time, I waited for the various saints' festivals. From Friday through Sunday night, the saint's statue or banner remained outside on a decorated altar. People visited with lighted candles and fresh flowers that they placed on the altar.

Crowds gathered near the bandstand, decorated with red, white, and blue banners. The amplifiers spread the music played by the Roma Band.

Poles erected along the sidewalks indicated the route of the Sunday procession. They decorated the poles with multicolored banners. Long scrolled wires with red, yellow, green and blue lights extended across the street from pole to pole.

Members of the organizations hosting the festivities carried the statue or saint's banner during the procession. We watched women with bare feet walk behind them. They recited the rosary and carried lighted candles. We admired the children dressed in white, First Communion outfits walking with them.

From Friday evening to Sunday evening, people gathered at the festival. Vendors of soft drinks, grilled sausages, fresh-opened clams, ice cream, slush and even balloons and trinkets, filled the area.

Our community supplied its immigrant residents and families with their daily needs. By making available the specialty items during holidays and festivities, the merchants made it possible for families to celebrate in the North End the traditions brought from their homeland.

BARGAINING

When Vincenzo, a door-to-door salesman, walked into our bakery in Boston's North End, Mama asked, "Che vendi oggi, cosi buoni?" (What are you selling today, anything good)?

He smiled proudly as he opened the large black suitcase he placed on Papa's desk. Mama and some of the women in the store gathered around to scrutinize the merchandise. He knew they were familiar with European open-cutwork embroidery on fine linen. Some had become skilled in this craft in their Italian homeland.

"Quanto, Vincenzo?" (How much, Vincenzo)? Mama asked as she picked out a linen tablecloth. Price was important.

Mama disliked the price quoted. "We can buy it for less on Hanover Street," she and the others said.

"But this comes from Spain," Vincenzo said. "Magnifico lavoro!" (Beautiful works)!

The women expected bargain prices from Vincenzo because he had less overhead expenses than the local merchants did. He bickered with Mama and the women, reminding them of his willingness to collect as little as twenty-five cents a week. Of course, a weekly visit to their home gave him an opportunity for another sale. But that day, no one purchased anything.

Bargaining was a daily part of buying in our Italian community. People bargained with the produce vendor, fish peddler, hardware merchant, shoemaker, the baker and even the barber.

"Joe, I'll bring all the kids tomorrow," some customers told the barber. "You give me two haircuts for the price of one—okay?"

During the fall and summer months, Vincenzo traveled through all the streets of Boston with his pushcart. He even ventured to East Boston via the ferry. Various sizes and colors of stockings and underwear hung from a makeshift wooden canopy attached to the sides of the pushcart. My friends and I giggled and pointed to the articles. We waited to catch what might fall. But, Vincenzo kept close watch on his merchandise.

Josie and Anna called to him from kitchen windows of their apartments. "Vincenzo, aspetta." (Vincenzo, wait). He waited for them to join the others on the street.

"How much?" Josie asked as she picked up a pair of stockings.

"Trentacinque solde." (Thirty-five cents). Vincenzo replied.

She frowned at his reply. "I'll pay you fifty cents for two pairs. That's all," she said firmly.

Vincenzo displayed anger but saw the opportunity to sell to those watching. "You make me lose money," he complained, taking fifty cents each from Josie and Anna. He completed three additional sales at the same price, before proceeding down Charter Street.

Jewish, Greek, Italian, and Irish merchants catered to the bargainers. During the depression years, they helped many families who preferred shopping in their North End community for day-to-day family needs.

"Come with me to Joe Shuman's." Mama often said. She purchased her sewing fabrics and supplies there.

I enjoyed going to his store on Hanover Street. While Mama checked for the prices of the various bolts of cotton, I looked around at all the other items. I yearned to have her purchase a pair of socks, a tam or beret I saw on display. But Mama's interest was only in the bolts of material and thread she needed. Mr. Shuman smiled patiently.

"I have some new yarn, Lucy," he said, knowing Mama loved to knit. He took a box of yarn from the shelf, removed the cover and placed it on the counter. But Mama only wanted her thread and material. In her calculated manner, she managed to get a five-or ten-cent reduction in the materials she purchased.

Whenever Mama and I visited Clayman's apparel shop on Salem Street, she waited for Lillian to approach her. Lillian recognized familiar faces of customers and immediately asked about the family.

Boxes filled the shelves of the narrow, compact store. A four-foot long counter separated the customers from the clerks. We saw folded bedspreads, infant and children's clothes, housedresses, and tablecloths displayed on hangers overhead and on the wall behind us. I stood next to Mama and watched Lillian's arms scan the boxes on the shelves for Mama's requested item. With her somber face, Lillian skillfully moved from one customer to another, serving two or three individuals consecutively. She allowed each an opportunity to think about the price quoted before returning.

Mama and the others knew how to be patient, but the young children became restless. I sighed when Mama asked to see two or three more of the same article. "Do you have this in blue?" Lillian diligently searched the shelves again.

While Mama examined the items, I listened to other customers. Some raised their voices in anger, others bargained quietly. Some threatened never to return because of dissatisfaction, while others entered and filled the spaces at the counter. Back and forth Lillian walked, each time ready to stand by her employer's merchandise.

"Take it home, Lucy," Lillian instinctively said when she felt Mama really wanted to purchase that item. "Pay me a little each week." If Mama hesitated, Lillian added, "I'll hold it for you here, Lucy. Leave me fifty cents or a dollar."

Inventory and layaways rested on shelves in the small back room. The merchant's little record book for weekly payments was as handy as Vincenzo's.

Mama bought bed linens, tablecloths, and towels in this fashion. She stored some in her cedar chest. Then, I wondered why. I learned later that Italian women prepared for their daughter's trousseau early in the child's life. When I married, I received those bargained goods as gifts from my parents. They lasted many years.

When Mama said, "Come with me. We're going to look for a new coat for you today," I knew I was in for a major bargaining experience. We always started in Wolfe's Clothing Store on Salem Street. When we entered the store, Mama had a price in mind, and the merchant did also. That did not frighten Mama.

After the customary "How are you today, Lucy? What can I do for you?" Mama selected a few styles for me to try on.

The clerk, looking at us, asked, "Do you like it?"

I knew not to show enthusiasm yet. With each coat I tried on, Mama asked for the price, but never revealed her pleasure or displeasure. After four or five coats, I tried each on a second time. The clerk repeated the price, and added, "But for you, Lucy, I can give you this one for . . ." Of course, he quoted a lower price than the original. It became a theatrical performance. If Mama liked the coat, she started bargaining with seemingly endless offers and counteroffers. If she became displeased, she took the coat off me. She took my hand, and we walked to the door after two hours of negotiating.

"Lucy, where are you going? That's a good price. Let's talk," the clerk cried out.

Mama and I continued out onto the sidewalk with the clerk following, cajoling Mama to return. How embarrassing, I thought!

The farther we walked from the store, the less my chances were of going home with a new coat. We only reentered for more bargaining if Mama had her mind set on purchasing that coat. Otherwise, we moved onward to another store or returned home. Mama knew when to try again. Eventually, she purchased a coat at a price that pleased her.

I became aware of these experiences again many years later, before retiring. From my secretarial position at our Wilmington North Intermediate School, I was selected to be a member of the bargaining committee. After many meetings, we had failed to negotiate an agreeable contract for the teachers and the secretarial staff. An evening's mediation meeting extended into early morning hours. We found ourselves again unable to reach an agreement. About 3 A.M., I began to feel like I was in the coat store on Salem Street.

"They know how far they want to go," I said to a co-worker, "And we know what we want," she replied.

I sat back in my chair quietly and thought of my mother, saying to myself, things might be different if Mama were here.

THE BREAD-SLICING MACHINE

"Did I hear Papa say he's getting a slicing machine for the bakery?" I asked my brother Peter. "Why do we need a slicing machine?" It surprised me. In my mind, I only knew of bread sliced as we needed it. However, Peter explained that neatly packaged sliced bread was becoming a popular item in the stores.

"The bread we hear people calling 'American white bread' is what gave Pa the idea to do the same with our Italian bread," Peter said proudly. "We'll be the first Italian bread bakery here to have sliced bread." In the 1930s, there were at least twelve Italian bread bakeries in the small North End community. Are they all going to slice bread, I wondered.

Then came the dilemma of where to place our slicing machine. Mama didn't really want it in the workshop. "If I have to go in the workshop to slice a loaf of bread, I won't be able to see the cash register or know when someone comes into the store."

"You'll hear the bell on the door when someone opens it." Papa said.

Next day we watched curiously as the deliverymen carried the machine into the workshop.

"It's a secondhand slicer," Peter whispered to me. I stared at the long, awkward-looking metal machine. I saw the thin twenty or so tooth-edged blades and wondered how the bread got sliced.

Papa wanted it away from the view of customers. "It will be better in here, Lucy, until we learn how to operate it," he told Mama. Then he turned to Peter and me. "Every night after supper, I want the two of you to be here to slice the bread." Peter was thirteen and had violin lessons to practice plus homework to do everyday. Being a shy nine-year-old, I was discouraged from saying anything by Papa's stern command, though I also thought about the homework.

We watched our parents as they practiced the next day. They also learned to regulate the heat needed to seal the bread wrappers. That evening after supper, Papa placed five loaves of bread in the long, slanted metal tray that led the bread down to the blades. He turned on the switch. The roaring sound of the motor and of the silver blades dancing up and down filled the room. We couldn't hear each other speak.

I stood beside Mama at the other end of the machine. She guided the bread carefully as it came through the knives and onto the waxed sheet of paper. She neatly folded the wrapper around the bread and then slid it onto the heated metal plate. There the ends and bottom of the waxed sheet heated and sealed the wrapper around the loaf. Immediately the aroma of fresh bread being sliced was erased by the peculiar smell of melting wax. She allowed it to cool for a second and handed it to me. One large, five-tier metal rack stood beside me. I placed the bread on the rack carefully. I was fascinated with seeing our name, "Orlando," on the wrapper. Peter prepared the large cardboard boxes nearby in which to store the wrapped loaves from the rack.

The novelty of "sliced bread" spread through our neighborhood. It wasn't long before crowds gathered inside and outside the bakery for the nightly event. Little children worked their way through the crowd to be up front. Papa decided to move the slicing machine into the retail store. He never wanted many people in the workshop. Mama was delighted not to have to walk back and forth from the workshop to the cash register when a customer requested a sliced loaf during the day. The slicing machine replaced the potbellied stove at the half-wall that separated the retail store from the workshop.

Uncle Nino and one or two of Mama's brothers seemed to always be present during the bread slicing. They were experienced behind the counter, having helped out at other times. This prevented Mama from stopping if a customer had to be served in the evening. They also helped when Papa had to assist the bakers who continued making bread.

Peter and I sighed each night at the slow process of slicing the numerous loaves. Eventually, Peter got permission to have a few teenage cousins and friends alternate in helping him move the filled cardboard boxes into another room. From there they got loaded into the delivery trucks in the morning. It was like a neighborhood project, though our parents were careful not to have anyone but grown-ups handle the fresh bread before it was wrapped.

By 1941, the increased orders from home-delivery customers and store deliveries of sliced Italian bread kept us at the slicing machine for at least two hours each night. Peter and I had to plan our evening events around the hours needed to complete the slicing. There were very few exceptions, like when Peter had to play in the school orchestra for a school event, or when we had to attend a wedding reception or special family affair. The experienced uncles and cousins volunteered to replace us on such evenings.

My favorite memory of bread slicing is that of munching on tiny end pieces of sliced bread that Mama set aside because they were too small to wrap. Occasionally, she passed some out to those standing by, watching.

THE TELEPHONE

"We're going to have a telephone in the bakery." Papa said. That excited us. "When our supply of flour runs low, we can call in an order, Lucy, rather than wait for a salesman to come." Papa was always eager to bring new technologies of America into our lives.

Most families in Boston's North End could not afford a telephone during the Depression. Only a few businesses in our community had one in 1933.

From my bakery perch, I watched the serviceman install the tall, thin, black telephone. At the top I saw the mouthpiece in which to speak. Then I watched the serviceman hang the hearing device on the side. The telephone rested on the roll-top desk.

Salesmen continued to make their visits. When one quoted Papa a particular price that he liked, Papa proudly requested, "Can you call in my order and confirm that price for me, Fred?"

"I could not do that before," Papa told us at supper. He wanted Peter and me to be aware of the progress in the country, even if a depression existed.

Papa had come to America from Sicily alone at the age of fourteen to live with his maternal uncle. The Depression here did not scare him because he had come from a greater depression in his homeland. He spoke of his progress in America often: from laying railroad tracks at fifteen; to later becoming a baker and bread deliverer; to serving in the infantry during World War I for his new country; and then having the privilege of opening his own family business in Boston.

At first only a few people used our telephone. After a few

months, Mama noticed that more and more customers asked, "Lucy, can I use the phone for a minute?"

An increase in telephone use by people became apparent. I remember seeing the installation of telephone booths sprouting up on many city streets. The increase of telephone use in the bakery led to Papa's request for a pay phone.

I watched the telephone employee from my perch as he removed the tall, black telephone from the desk. Then he installed the pay phone on a wall clearing next to Papa's desk.

"It's a privilege to have a phone," Papa told us.

"But we had to make this change." Mama said. "It was costing the business too much."

"The phone will still be here for people to use." Papa said. The neighbors and customers quickly adjusted to the use of the pay telephone when they needed it.

Around 1935, Papa decided we needed a telephone in our apartment. After the experience in the bakery, he requested a pay phone to be installed. At first it embarrassed Peter and me. What are our friends going to say about a pay phone in our apartment, we both thought. Soon we learned that Papa had made the right decision. For a while, we became messengers to many in our apartment building. Then a parade of neighbors came to use the phone. When my brother's high school friends came home with him to work on projects, they called their home outside our community to inform their parents of their whereabouts. The pay phone proved to be worthwhile, especially when the telephone company allowed us to dial a code number to contact the bakery without charge.

I thought back to how we communicated in the neighborhood prior to the telephone. If Papa wanted Mama to return to the bakery, or if he wanted Peter or me, he used to stand outside on the sidewalk and whistle a familiar tune until we looked out the apartment window. If Mama wanted to contact Peter or me in our apartment, she called out our names from the sidewalk until we answered.

Somehow, everybody in the neighborhood became familiar

with their own family's "whistle" or calls. Occasionally, I put my head out the window when I heard a whistle or call, just to see if I was being paged. My friends said they did the same.

It wasn't until the World War II years, as the country moved out of the depression, that telephones became affordable to North End residents. I like to think that Papa always had faith that a telephone would someday be found in everyone's home.

THE PUPPET SHOW

"What can we make with this?" MaryAnn asked one day when we had completed a long braided cord hanging from the center of a spool. We learned this craft at the North Bennet Street Industrial School which we often attended after school.

My parents allowed Jennie, MaryAnn and me to play in the workshop of the family bakery when baking ended on Saturday afternoons. At ten years old the three of us enjoyed weaved long strips of yarn around four nails on the empty spools of thread. Papa placed the nails on the spools for us and Mama gave us colored yarn to use.

MaryAnn's question led me to think of my grandmother whom I often watched as she braided strips of material cut from old coats and jackets. Then she sewed the braids into rugs for her children.

"Why don't we sew these into little round rugs?" I asked.

Jennie added her idea of finding a cardboard box. "We can color windows and doors in it and make it into a dollhouse. We can make other things for it too," she said with excitement.

"Why don't we sew some dolls from old socks?" MaryAnn added. "They can be our puppets like the ones we saw at the North Bennet Street School."

"If we sew puppets, why don't we put on a show for the little kids?" Jennie asked. We became really excited with that thought.

"I'll go ask my grandfather for one of his large cardboard boxes." Her grandparents had a produce store across the street from the bakery.

What a great idea. We can place the little rugs on the floor of the puppet stage, I thought.

We talked about which fairytale to prepare for presentation to the children. MaryAnn suggested _Sleeping Beauty._ Jennie and I agreed.

"I'll ask my father if we can use the back room some Saturday afternoon for the show," I said. "We can use the Henchman Street door as the entrance. We won't need to have the kids come in from the front door on Charter Street."

The large room we hoped to use housed a second oven and was also used as a bread storage area. The delivery drivers took their orders for the day through the Henchman Street door early in the morning. That would give us a private area for our afternoon show.

Papa consented when I approached him with our idea. He was so eager to oblige that I wondered if he questioned our determination to complete our project.

The next thing for us to do was to search through our mother's rag box. Each of us was familiar with the collection of old clothes, tablecloths, sheets, and towels that our mothers used for mending or housecleaning. With the help of our imaginations and the materials available from these scrap boxes, we often became whatever we professed to be; either a seamstress, a doctor, nurse, dentist, teacher, or mother. After our search we found the materials to successfully complete our puppets.

MaryAnn had two younger sisters; Jennie had a younger brother and two sisters; and I had younger cousins nearby. We told them about our puppet show and asked them to spread the word to their playmates.

My friends and I met several times a week to focus on the story of Sleeping Beauty. We wrote our version to be presented with only two characters - Sleeping Beauty and the Prince. The braids from our spools became three little round rugs on the floor of the cardboard stage. We painted a small empty candy box yellow and used it as Sleeping Beauty's bed.

While Jennie decided what colorful cloth to use as the curtain for our stage, MaryAnn cut a crown out of white craft paper and colored it with yellow crayon. She measured it to the head of the Prince. With glue MaryAnn secured the crown to his head.

When we completed the puppets and the stage, I asked, "How will we work these puppets?" During the time we sewed the puppets and prepared the cardboard box as our stage area we had never thought about how to do the actual performance. MaryAnn thought of a great solution.

"We'll split two clothespins in half," she said. "We'll sew string to the hands of the puppets and tie the other end of the string to half of the clothespin. We'll use the other clothespin half to do the same with the heads."

Moving the puppets seemed like an easy procedure when we watched other puppeteers perform the task. However, we realized that we had much practicing to do. Our determination to succeed led us to practicing our lines each day until we learned to move the puppets properly. Jennie became our director and stage manager, opening and closing the curtain. Several weeks passed before we felt ready to give our performance.

The children displayed great enthusiasm when we announced our performance date. We told them they had to pay one cent to see the puppet show.

On that day, MaryAnn and I nervously prepared the puppets and the stage while Jennie greeted the children at the Henchman Street door and collected their pennies. About fifteen children made themselves comfortable on the wooden floor. They sat facing the stage which rested on top of several turned over bread boxes.

Jennie heard them express excitement at the prospects of receiving free candy during intermission. How did this rumor start? We had never mentioned serving candy to the children.

The three of us discussed it for a minute. Then we decided to buy candy with the money to avoid receiving a scolding from our parents for charging the children.

Jennie quickly ran to Peppie's Candy Store nearby. She returned with enough candy for our audience.

While MaryAnn lowered the Prince and I lowered Sleeping Beauty onto the stage, Jennie quieted the audience and slowly pulled the string that opened the curtain. We proceeded with our puppet show.

The smiling faces of the children as they ate their candy during intermission and their enthusiastic applause at the conclusion made that entire activity a special day to remember.

A DIFFERENT HALLOWEEN

In October 1931, our family had adjusted well to living with Aunt Paola, Papa's eldest sister, and husband, Uncle Tony, in Salemi, Sicily. We had arrived in September.

My brother Peter and I began to think of Halloween. As first-generation Americans, we heard little about Halloween at home; but in school our teachers taught us to make masks and little baskets from construction paper. I remembered receiving jellybeans from our teacher on Halloween Day to place in our basket. After school, we visited the local merchants and cried, "Trick or Treat" in hopes of receiving more candy.

"Pa, do they celebrate Halloween here?" we asked.

"No," Papa replied. "They celebrate something different on the eve of All Souls Day."

"What?" we asked.

"La notte delle morte." (the night of the dead), Uncle Tony said.

Uncle Tony sat next to Papa listening to our conversation. He understood English because he had spent some time in the United States with us while he worked in Boston as a laborer.

Being four years older than me, Peter knew about All Saints Day and All Souls Day from Sunday school classes. I became quiet at the sound of "the dead."

"On the evening of November first, you'll place your shoes on the floor inside the entrance door," Uncle Tony explained.

"Perche?"

"Nella mattina trovati una sopressa." (In the morning, you will find a surprise).

The thought of a surprise lit up our faces with smiles. We waited anxiously.

Peter had turned eleven in July, and I was six years old when we departed by ocean liner for Sicily. The purpose of the visit was to meet Papa's mother and his two married sisters and their families. Papa had not seen any of them in twenty-four years. Mama also had relatives in the same village that she hadn't seen for many years.

Aunt Paola and Uncle Tony made our stay in Salemi, Sicily, very comfortable. Few people in the town had a toilet facility and running water in their homes as they did. Uncle Tony had sacrificed living and working in Boston to make it possible for him to pay for these conveniences for his family.

During our stay, we learned that our parents had grown up celebrating "La festa delli morti."

Mama explained that on the eve of All Souls' Day, deceased relatives visit during the night to leave gifts for well-behaved children.

Peter smiled happily, but I became frightened again. I found it difficult to go to sleep that night. Thoughts of dead relatives visiting during the night became unnerving. I lay quietly on my straw bed thinking about Santa Claus.

I remembered my first-grade teacher reading us the long poem, "'Twas the Night Before Christmas." Christmas is in December, and this is November, I mumbled to myself. Confused but eager to receive a gift, I fell asleep finally while concentrating on what the surprise might be.

Peter awakened me early that morning. We ran down the loft stairs and to the door. Each of us found a small paper bag resting beside our shoes. I quickly opened mine. To my delight, I found a small pastel-colored marzipan doll and miniature marzipan fruit.

Peter laughed loudly at the sight of his small marzipan donkey. Each day, Peter had tormented Uncle Tony about taking the family donkey out for a ride.

"Now you have your own." Uncle Tony teased.

On Halloween each year, I remember the different celebration Peter and I experienced in Salemi, Sicily in 1931.

NORTH BENNET STREET
INDUSTRIAL SCHOOL

Our Community Center

The school bell rang, and our thoughts quickly switched from studying to playing. We gathered in the rear of the classroom to put on our coats and hats. MaryAnn whispered, "Are you going to the North Bennet School today?"

I nodded. "Are you stopping for a pickle?" I asked.

"No I'm buying candy," she said.

Already my mouth watered with the thought of the juicy, vinegary pickle. As we left the elementary school, MaryAnn, Jennie, Cousin Josie and I followed classmates a short distance to the candy store on North Bennet Street. The store owner watched as we selected the pickle of our choice from the barrel near the door. His wife served MaryAnn and others at the counter.

There were those who couldn't buy, but waited for us to offer some of our pickle or candy. Each time the teeth of a friend crunched out a portion of my pickle, I felt the water increase in my mouth. I waited for my turn. By the time we walked the two or three hundred yards up North Bennet Street to the Industrial School, our candy or pickle was finished.

We reached up from the wide, single doorstep, pulled open the tall, green double doors, and climbed the four or five wooden steps to the first floor. The warm heat of the building embraced us on cold winter days. The smell of fresh wood shavings or wood stain, blending with the aromas of various foods from the kitchen was familiar to us. We made our way into the large game room facing the stairway.

We removed our coats and scrambled for seats at one of the large wooden tables in the room. The school, in existence since 1885 at this site, provided vocational courses like the art of making and repairing violins and other instruments, making and repairing furniture as well as courses in cobbling, printing, carpentry and cooking. The need to teach immigrant women without special skills how to operate sewing machines led to sewing classes for young and older women. This helped them to find employment in the garment industry in Boston. To the children like myself it became our community center where we enrolled in tap dancing, drama, chorus, basket weaving, sewing and craft classes.

We found the shelves along the walls of the game room filled with games like Tiddlywinks, Pick-Up Sticks, Jacks, Dominoes and Checkers. With each visit we sat to decide what we wanted to play. Those interested in Ping-Pong walked towards the back of the room to play at those tables. Jennie, MaryAnn, Josie and I decided to play Tiddlywinks.

Volunteers helped Mrs. Gomez supervise the game room until we reported to our classrooms at the appointed time. Boys and girls attended separate classes on separate days. Sometimes we signed up for the craft classes or basket weaving, but my favorite choices were drama and dancing. The numerous musical movies of the day influenced my friends and me to select Tap Dancing and Ballet Classes. We dreamed of imitating Ruby Keeler, Dick Powell, Bill Robinson, Shirley Temple, Buddy Ebson, Mickey Rooney, and Judy Garland.

Miss Hamel taught us to sing as a group and tap dance to "Side by Side" and "On the Sidewalks of New York." We tried desperately to stand on our toes during ballet sessions. It was fun learning the routines. In the summer we taught them to the neighborhood children. How proud we felt when mothers watched us from their windows during performances in the Goodrich Alley courtyard.

Christmas was an exciting time at the North Bennet Street

School. Several classes prepared for the Christmas performances and Christmas party held in the auditorium.

I remember being a shepherd when I was about eight or nine years old. I wore the costume my mother helped sew for me. I clutched my staff and made my way across the stage with the other shepherds. We stopped at the manger while everyone in the audience sang Christmas carols, including instructors and volunteers. After the performance, they treated us with cookies and ice cream. We departed with a small box of Christmas hard candy. Then we all looked forward to the Christmas school vacation.

Though we visited the game room during that week's vacation, we anxiously waited to bring in our money for the second session of classes. The exciting moment came when the instructor announced that a Minstrel Show would take place in late spring. All students of the Community Center could participate.

Like my Cousin Josie and friends, I looked forward to spending time at the Center, especially during the winter. Apartments were small, and we had to rely on the streets for play area. This was a congenial place to meet a few times a week and participate in various activities.

I remember that some of my friends attended the one or two weeks of camping in Boxford, Massachusetts, but I never attended. Another program offered by the Community Center was for boys to attend Caddy Camp at various golf courses in Massachusetts and New Hampshire.

One important performance during my attendance in the dance class beside the Minstrel Shows was the German dance done ballet style in our bare feet. Dolly, a neighbor of mine, was selected as the lead dancer in my group.

I was about eleven years old at the time. Miss Hamel informed us during a rehearsal that we had been invited to perform at the Esplanade on the Charles for a special spring occasion. Though the Esplanade is in the West End close to the North End, many of the young children had never been in that area. To those who hadn't, leaving the North End became as exciting as a trip to another state.

Enthusiasm grew in the group because we had been selected to perform for "strangers." On that special day, a bus transported us to the Esplanade with our costumes in hand. Fashionably dressed women welcomed us with smiles. They ushered us into the dressing room, put on our make up, while others helped with the costumes. I felt like a princess that day with all the attention received from these kind "strangers."

At the proper time, Dolly gracefully danced onto the stage with the rhythm of the music. We slowly entered behind her. Our silky costumes moved gently in the spring air with every movement we made. My heart pounded as I counted the steps to myself, anxious not to make a mistake. I hardly noticed that I was dancing barefoot on an open-air stage. The loud applause at the end broke my concentration. I murmured it's over! Then I bowed with the others. Our eyes filled with tears as the clapping continued. We returned to center stage for our second bow and then ran downstairs into the dressing room. We hugged each other and the instructor as we chatted with excitement. We rushed to change. What impressed me the most was the number of people who remained in the foyer. They waited to congratulate us as we left the dressing room and headed for the bus that brought us back to the Community Center.

MaryAnn, Jennie, Josie and I continued attending classes there until we became teenagers. Then our interest turned to the Friday night dances for boys and girls at the Center. Many of us remained active as volunteers in preparation for the annual Minstrel Shows. With each show, we relived the experiences of exhaustion and frustration during rehearsals. We persevered through costume selections, make up decisions, and dress rehearsals to arrive at the day of the performance. The reward each time was the applause that filled the auditorium of the Community Center just as it did for us when we were the young troupers on stage.

Paul Revere Mall " The Prado" across the street from St. Stephen's Church

Paul Revere Mall plaque. Adjacent to the fountain.

Vita and Williams's grandchildren visiting "The Fountain" at the Paul Revere Mall. The Old North Church is in the background.

PAUL REVERE

Excitement filled the room when Miss Barry, our fourth-grade teacher, told our class, "We are going to practice singing for the spring dedication of the Paul Revere Mall."

For months, in the 1930s, we had watched construction workers on our way to and from school as they demolished old buildings on Hanover, Charter and Unity Streets. Also to be built alongside the mall was a new Elliot Elementary School and a larger fire station for the community.

On the mall's dedication day, teachers and students walked to the area from the Hancock and Paul Revere Schools on Prince Street and the Christopher Columbus School on Tileston Street. We entered through the Unity Street entrance, opposite the rear gate of the Old North Church.

"Girls, we'll line up here to the left of the fountain," Miss Barry said.

The large, round, cement water fountain, with a visible spout at its center, attracted our attention. We expected to see water sprouting high from its center, but it did not happen that day.

My classmates, Jennie, MaryAnn, Cousin Josie and I huddled together as the cool spring breeze blew around us.

It pleased us to watch the newly planted trees sway with the light breeze. We had few trees in our community.

As officials filled the podium near the fountain, crowds gathered around us. We listened to a dignitary who pointed to a plaque on the brick wall. He explained that Christopher Stanley, a resident of the North End, donated the land to Boston in 1830 for the purpose of constructing a free school for children to attend. Paul Revere and his friends had attended the North Writing School on Love Lane, one street away. Love Lane became Tileston Street in later years in honor of Mr. Tileston, who had been the school's headmaster.

"Paul Revere frequently passed through this area," the speaker said. "He attended services at the Old North Church with his young friends, and they became bell ringers for the church."

It pleased us to hear that Paul Revere, in later years, had moved his family from North Square, a few blocks from the mall, to a home near the corner of Charter and Hanover Street. He lived there until his death in 1840.

Our eyes opened wide as we heard another speaker mention the song we had been practicing to sing.

The speaker told us, "A resident of the North End, Samuel Francis Smith, wrote a poem in the 1800s called 'America.' Eventually a composer added music to the poem."

Now we knew why Miss Barry chose that song. Upon the signal from the podium, she gave us our pitch. We proudly sang, "My country 'tis of thee . . ." People looking out their windows and the crowd in the mall rewarded us with applause.

"We'll follow the people to the other end of the mall," Miss Barry said, as the dignitaries began leaving the podium. "Let's keep together, girls, two by two."

We moved toward the Hanover Street entrance and stood near the covered monument.

Someone gave a brief speech. Then we watched the unveiling of the beautiful life-size sculpture of Paul Revere mounted on his horse. It faces Hanover Street.

I remember that we sang, "Oh beautiful for spacious skies . . ." as loud as we could with great pride.

The Paul Revere Mall became a daily gathering place for the Italian residence. They quickly renamed it "The Prado" —their Italian word for meeting or gathering area. People sat on the cement benches among the trees to read newspapers, or to chat with friends. Elderly men came with wooden crates for a table, stools, and playing cards. They played their favorite "Briscula" (Polka) for hours.

On our way home from school, we saw young mothers in the park visiting with friends while their babies napped in their carriages.

Our fascination with the water spraying in the fountain caused us to visit The Prado each day on our way home from school. Later the water became a danger to young children climbing into the fountain. The city officials shut off the water for a number of years. But we remained attracted to the fountain. We found ourselves climbing into the empty, large, gray cement structure and running around a few times before walking home.

On April 18, after supper, my friends and I usually stood in front of the Old North Church on Salem Street. We watched invited guests enter for the annual Patriots' Day memorial services. Many of us had learned in school about the significance of the two lanterns placed in the steeple that evening — "One if by land, and two if by sea."

The next morning, we met at the Prado near Paul Revere's statue. We watched two gentlemen dressed in colorful colonial attire. They represented Paul Revere and William Dawes. Each year, descendants of Revere and Dawes reenacted the ride immortalized in Longfellow's poem. In April 18, 1774, Revere and Dawes had ridden through Charlestown, Cambridge, Concord and Lexington to warn everyone that the British were coming by sea. This was the official beginning of the Revolutionary War.

Our eyes never wandered far from the two descendants of Revere and Dawes. They tried desperately to keep the horses calm in the crowded street. After introductions by a city official, we watched the two men riding swiftly up Hanover Street until they disappeared from sight.

We walked slowly back to our playing area on Charter Street across from Papa's bakery to wait for tour buses. They arrived every few hours and parked where we played. As the tourists exited, we joined them on the short walk around the corner to the Old North Church. I walked along with them and soon learned to recite the brief history of Paul Revere that my brother and others recited to all the tourists.

"Paul Revere was married twice, had sixteen children — eleven boys and five girls. On the door of his house there's 144 hand-made spikes. The last three spikes were taken off by the British. Right beside the door of his home stands the old hitching post. That's where Paul Revere tied his horse. The Horse kicked the bottom, bit the top and ran away three times.

On the roof of the house were four chimneys. The last two were taken off by the British. The half moons were carved by Paul Revere. The windows were stained by the sun — came all the way from England. Paul Revere was so many kinds of smiths that the people in Boston called him Mr. Smith. He was a blacksmith, tinsmith, coppersmith, goldsmith, silversmith, and a dentist. He was the first to make a set of wooden false teeth for General Washington and General Joseph Warren . . ."

After the recitations we returned to wait near the buses, hoping to catch a few pennies from the tourists when the buses departed.

My friends and I talked often about Paul Revere having walked the same streets we walked. Sometimes, when I closed my eyes, I felt like I could almost see him riding by us on his horse. I wondered, what would he think about seeing children of Italian immigrants living in his "North Boston" and reciting his history?

RECYCLING

I learned about recycling early in life by watching Mama show customers in our Boston North End bakery how to cut open the sides and bottoms of empty flour bags.

"Cusa quatro insiami e ti fai uno linsolo." (Sew four together and you'll have a bed sheet) Mama said.

"Grazie, grazie, Lucia. We do watta you say," they replied thankfully.

Mama felt obliged during the Great Depression to share the excess flour and salt sacks accumulating in the bakery. She disliked wasting anything.

Each time Papa ordered flour for his bread-baking business, it arrived by train and was stored in a Charlestown warehouse. Several days later, I saw the Petringa or Stella men arrive in their delivery truck, wearing white caps and handkerchiefs tied around their necks. I climbed onto my perch, on the wooden icebox, to watch each man lift a cotton sack of flour onto his shoulder. They layered them crisscross, two by two, in a ten-foot square area of the workshop.

Mama offered them a drink as they stopped to wipe their flour-covered faces and necks before departing. Later that day they returned to deliver large cotton sacks of sugar and 50-pound bags of salt. They also brought shortening and malt in cardboard or metal containers. Sesame seeds arrived in bulging three-foot burlap bags.

I did not enjoy watching Papa open those burlap sacks. By snipping and pulling the top threads of the bag, burlap scent and dust sprayed from the sack, causing me to sneeze as he poured the contents into a wooden barrel.

Papa and the bakers stored emptied flour and salt bags in separate wooden barrels. The flour sacks became linings for the wide wooden bread boxes in which rolled bread dough raised.

Mama checked the barrels weekly, removing any soiled flour bags. She took them home and soaked them in the soapstone sink. Later she placed them in a large metal basin and boiled them on the coal stove. To remove stubborn print, she added bleach during her second boiling.

The flour bags returned to the bakery remade into aprons by Mama. She fashioned her pattern by centering the King Arthur, Gold Medal, and Northern Flour logos on the apron fronts. They received daily use in the bakery and in our home. I have as a memento one of Mama's aprons. The words NORTHERN FLOUR are still visible.

I saw Mama and Aunt Lena sew the material into sheets, pillowcases and table napkins. They decorated the pillow cases with their hand, crocheted lace, and sometimes embroidered monograms on a corner of the napkins.

Mama encouraged other mothers to sew soft-cotton petticoats from the material, as she did for me. Remaining pieces of material became washcloths or dust-and-dry mopping cloths.

"Lena, use these for hand or dish towels," Mama said to Aunt Lena when she gave her laundered salt sacks.

As spring approached, many housewives saved emptied tomato cans to start seedlings. Customers asked Papa for empty metal shortening or malt containers. Soon we saw miniature gardens of basil, parsley, tomato, pepper, squash, eggplant or cucumber plants growing in a variety of containers. Emptied wooden barrels, sawed in half, became recipients of miniature lime, orange or fig trees. In our community with little vegetation existing, we welcomed their sight on our fire escapes and on the roof every spring and summer.

Younger cousins or needy families became recipients of our outgrown clothing. Unusable jackets, pants, coats, including worn drapes and bedspreads went to Nonna, my maternal grandmother. Nonna lived a few doors away from our bakery. Her specialty was making hand-braided rugs. Each of her nine children brought her their old clothes. She carefully removed all buttons and snaps. She added these to her collection stored in a large cookie canister. Nonna cut the material into three-inch-long strips and stored them in an empty laundered burlap or flour bag.

I enjoyed bringing Nonna her daily fresh loaf of bread, especially in the winter. She treated me to a slice of bread and butter, sprinkled with sugar, that she toasted in the coal-stove oven. She served it with hot cocoa.

While eating, I sat watching her work a few feet away, close to a large window. Nonna took advantage of the light shining into her third-floor apartment. I saw her run a piece of thread over a yellowed ball of bee's wax before threading her needle.

"Che fai, Nonna?" (What are you doing?) I inquired.

"Rinforzo lo filo," (I am strengthening the thread) she replied.

Nonna sewed the long strips together until an ample supply gathered at her feet. Then she wove three individual strips into a braid. It amazed me to see how she creatively arranged her beautiful color schemes into oblong-or round-shaped rugs. The rugs became children and grandchildren's treasured gifts from Nonna.

Recycling became a necessity during the Depression because of the unemployment predicament of many families. The average family in our neighborhood consisted of four or more children. To extend the life of clothing, mothers sewed patches over worn spots. They also learned how to turn worn shirt collars.

I remember Mama, Aunt Lena, and Nonna sitting together in our kitchen removing collars. They folded the worn side inward. They sewed the "turned" collar back into the shirt on Mama's Singer pedal sewing machine. Some of our neighbors did the sewing by hand. I saw salvageable cotton cloth from shirts or sheets become handkerchiefs or panties for little girls.

On rainy or snow days, wooden floors, sidewalks and door entrances received a dusting of recycled wood shavings purchased from sawmills. Papa and the local merchants kept a supply on hand. It kept floors from becoming slippery.

My brother Peter's chore on snowy days was to clean a path

on the sidewalk. I followed him with a broom and swept the snow off our wide granite entrance. Peter piled the removed sidewalk snow along the curbstone. Sometimes he mischievously tossed some out over the hardened snow in the middle of the road, which led to an unusual recycling moment.

We waited anxiously for a horse-drawn wagon to see the imprints in the snow left by the horse's hoofs and thin wooden wagon wheels. But I found that my twelve-year-old brother and his friends had more in mind.

As horses slowly maneuvered around the corner of Salem Street and down our hilly Charter Street, inevitably one slipped on the loose powdery snow. His hind legs buckled under him and he sat on the snow bewildered. Children gathered quickly. They joined Peter and his friends in giggling and laughing. But it saddened me to watch the struggling horse. Neighbors ran to help the wagon master.

It scared me to hear the frenzied animal struggle and neigh fiercely. I was especially frightened when I saw the sudden burst of vapors from his nostrils as he finally stood up and shook his mane. I smiled when the wagon master prepared to move down the hill again. Peter and his friends jeered and laughed as they saw the excited horse leave a large "dung" on the street. It did not remain there long. Someone quickly appeared with a shovel and container to make use of it as fertilizer. That was the ultimate in recycling.

GAMES WE PLAYED

The Roof Was Our Penthouse; the Street Was Our Playground

"Your friends are on the roof today," Mama said.

"Oh, good," I said, taking it as an invitation for me to join my friends.

Sometimes, we gathered on the roof to play house. One of us chose to play mother, one to be father and another to play nurse or doctor. Little brothers and sisters became our children. Some days we played school. We became teachers and the younger siblings became our students. I enjoyed the time in the open air above the street especially during the summer. On very hot days, we took an old blanket with us to the roof so we could sunbathe. We enjoyed the peace and quiet on the roof without the noise of horse-drawn wagons, peddlers with pushcarts calling out their wares. It was great being a distance away from the loud automobile horns honking for us to get off the street. We retreated to the roof when we wanted to escape from the odor of garbage on garbage-collection days. We pretended that being on the roof transported us into a different world.

One of the things I enjoyed was when Mama and some of the other mothers taught us how to pull threads from the edges of square linen pieces. They taught us to make fringed napkins. Sometimes we worked on all four sides of the piece, sometimes on only two sides. It was a time to work outdoors and converse with our friends. We were proud of what we accomplished, especially when the napkins appeared at the dinner table. Our parents were happy because they knew where we were.

On a sunny winter day, I loved accompanying Mama to the roof while she hung her laundry to dry. The clean, crisp air under a blue sky and shining sun made me forget for a few moments that we lived in a crowded community. After a snowstorm, I remember being anxious to see the beautiful white snow on the roof that looked like mounds of white cotton. The boards of the three-foot fence along the edges of the roof were edged in snow. Looking towards the building across the street and seeing snow stuck to the red bricks made me feel I was somewhere in a quiet, serene country town. We loved jumping into the snow. At times we made a snowman for the young children to enjoy. They helped us put a carrot in its face for a nose. We looked for an old scarf to wrap around its neck. I liked making a snowman on the roof because it never remained very clean or lasted too long on sidewalks.

As teenagers, we gathered on the roof with friends to exchange thoughts about movies we had seen and our views and feelings about boys we liked.

We were not alone though, because I knew that my brother and some of his teenage friends used the roof as a private smoking area, hoping a neighbor would not see or tell on them.

In the summer, we had prankish boys who liked to scare the girls. They filled paper bags or balloons with water. They tossed them off the roof and onto the street. We scrambled for cover. That caused an outburst of anger from the elders sitting out on the sidewalks. The boys quickly jumped from one roof to another to avoid apprehension. They appeared a short time later exiting from a building a distance away. Somehow we always guessed at who the pranksters were, but everyone remained silent.

Many boys who loved pigeons built a home for their pigeons out on the roof. Some even raced them, letting them fly from their coop and waited for their safe return. They spent time cleaning the coops, feeding the pigeons and training them to race. For many of us, the roof was our private penthouse.

We also loved playing on the sidewalk or street. Boys and girls created games of our own like tossing playing cards or baseball cards towards a wall. The person getting the card closest to the wall became the winner. If someone tossed a "leaner," (a card to lean up against a wall) he or she became an instant winner. The winner kept all the cards played. A tie resulted in a playoff. The rules we set forth governed this type of game played with cards or pennies.

I remember running to Peppie's Candy Store many times with my friends after collecting milk or tonic bottles. Peppie took the bottles and gave us pennies that we pitched in our game.

After a game of tossing baseball cards, the boys gathered to bargain with others, offering two or three lesser-known ballplayers' cards for one special Joe DiMaggio card. Sometimes tempers flared, and a neighbor watching the exchange came over to calm the situation.

A favorite game in the spring and summer was playing with marbles. MaryAnn, Jennie and I each had a collection that we tried to keep hidden from our brothers. One day we watched the ingenious boys take a piece of nine-by-twelve-inch cardboard from which they cut out an arch. Then they leaned it up against the brick wall. Immediately, we decided to do the same, only we went to a spot across the street. It was fun rolling the marble hoping to get it through the arched space and be a winner. However, I don't remember being as anxious as Peter and his friends about bargaining with others. They wanted to exchange three or four marbles for an "aggie." Actually, I never understood the difference between a marble and an aggie.

Boys and girls both collected bottle caps. We spent hours in the summer sitting on the steps of doorways or in corridors, placing the cap cork side up. One at a time, the players tried to flip the caps over with the index finger. If it turned, that was a win that we added to our collection.

The boys had another use for some of their bottle caps. They flipped out the thin layer of cork from the underside. Beanie caps were very popular in the 'thirties. The boys forced the fabric of the beanie cap between the cork and metal cap. They did this to shirts also. But mothers soon put a stop to that because the shirt with the cap was difficult to launder.

With our pennies from returning milk and tonic bottles, we also bought a ball attached with elastic to a thin wooden paddle. When the elastic detached from the paddle, we made use of the items by drawing a chalk line on the sidewalk or street. We hit the ball back and forth over the line and called ourselves "ping-pong players."

One of my favorite items purchased with my pennies was a top. I was jealous that my brother could spin his top so well. I made him show me how to spin mine. We became competitors not only with the top but also with the yo-yo purchased for a few pennies. But I never mastered the art of using the yo-yo like Peter did.

In the spring, when I heard the boys hammering nails into wooden boxes I realized they might be making scooters. The boys easily unscrewed and separated a roller skate into two portions. Then they attached two wheels of the skate to the front and two wheels to the back of a footboard. Next they attached a wooden box to one end of the footboard and a scooter was born. The boys decorated their scooters with bottle caps and colorful pieces of cloth to wave in the air as they rode their scooters. Sometimes they even spelled out their initials on the scooter with the bottle caps.

I enjoyed my skates with my friends either at the Slye Park across from the Copp's Hill Burying Ground or just skating up and down the red-brick sidewalk. I wasn't allowed to skate in the street, though Peter and the older boys did.

Spring, summer and fall was a good time to play roleevio, tin can, and "buck, buck, how many fingers up," each on our own little turf on the street.

When the boys tried to break into our jump rope in an attempt to take over our street area, my older cousins and friends interceded. They challenged the boys to double Dutch or "peppers." That often resulted in the boys leaving. We stayed in our territory and the boys moved down the street to set up their baseball game.

The sound of the broomstick or makeshift wooden bat echoed through the area. It was inevitable that the hollow, pimpled, rubber ball would shatter a window at one time or another. But for the most part, we enjoyed the games almost daily during the spring, summer and fall.

"Wanna be an outfielder?" we sometimes heard from our older brothers.

"Yes!" we screamed as we ran down behind their designated second base. Soon we realized why they wanted us in the game. They had become tired of chasing the ball down the street. Because of our delight at being participants, we stayed in the game. When we became ten and twelve years old, we likewise enticed our younger siblings to play outfielders in the same way.

Part of the fun of thinking about old times is remembering the enjoyable times on the roof, on the sidewalks and street.

I KNEW IT WAS SPRING

The three-foot mounds of hardened snow along the curbstones became our private paths during winters in the North End of Boston. They slowly melted into the sewers, as days grew warmer. Mama opened the kitchen windows slightly to let warm air into our apartment at 38 Charter Street.

The streets of our Italian community were very quiet late at night and early in the morning. When I heard familiar noises like the clattering sound of horses' hoofs and tinkling milk bottles on the milk wagon, I knew it was spring. I heard the early morning calls from the iceman bellowing, "I EEE SSSS." He waited for someone like Mama to call out the window, "Tony, gimme twenty-five cents today."

He chipped out a piece with his ice pick, lifted it with his tongs and delivered it right into our icebox. He had to climb four flights of stairs for twenty-five cents.

The voices of excited children and the noise of hammers outside brought me to the window one Saturday morning. I looked out and saw my brother Peter, Billy Peri, Gasper "Red," Paulie Grasso, Sonny and a few other boys breaking up some wooden crates.

I was excited as I followed Mama down the four flights of stairs a few minutes later. She went across the street to help Papa in the family's bakery, and I stayed on the sidewalk with my friend MaryAnn, Gasper's sister.

Mary and Nettie (Sonny's sisters) sat with me on the doorstep. Soon Jennie joined us. They lived in the same apartment building with me.

We watched the boys in front of the building who separated

slats from long orange create. They were preparing to build scooters.

They got their boxes from Tony Beninati and Harry Dorfman's grocery stores. The orange crates came from Jennie's grandfather Zio Aspero Beninati's produce store in the stoop of our apartment building.

I watched Peter nail one roller skate to each end of a sturdy board. Some boys used half a skate for each end. Then Peter placed an empty wooden box upright on top of the end of the board. He nailed the box to the board with the open end of the box facing the rider.

"Hold this here," he said as he handed me a narrow slat about two feet long. Then he placed it on top of the box and secured it with a few nails.

"This will be my handlebar," he said.

Peter and the boys had their collection of bottle caps with them. My girl friends and I passed them out to the boys who added them to the fronts and tops of the crates as decorations. Some boys added a few strips of colorful material to the sides of the crates or attached an old bicycle horn to their handmade vehicle. Each scooter received a loud cheer from the onlookers.

"Can I have a ride, can I have a ride?" I asked Peter.

"I have to try it first," he replied. He took off down the street a short distance, turned into Henchman Street to stop, and then returned to where I stood.

"Stay on the sidewalk," he said as he handed me the scooter, "and go slow," he commanded.

I followed his instructions and traveled only a short distance. I enjoyed my ride.

All day the children maneuvered over the red-brick sidewalk and cobblestone street. It only took a few bumps and dumps before even the youngest boys or girls mastered the scooter ride.

The noisy vehicles did not appeal to the adults, but delighted the children who had waited all winter to build their scooters.

I knew it was spring when the neighbors uncovered their half-barrels and boxes kept on the fire escapes or on the roof.

They planted parsley, basil, scallions, tomatoes, various peppers and flower seeds in their containers.

The small bedrooms and kitchens of most apartments provided little playing area. Few people had or could afford a living room in our community during the Great Depression.

We climbed out a bedroom or kitchen window and sat on boxes on the fire escape where we met with our friends when weather permitted. Sometimes we played on the roof and imagined it to be our penthouse.

Tenant owners of boxed gardens warned us about playing too close to their plants.

"If I see you near those plants, I'll tell your mother *and* your father." We knew they meant it.

By the middle of May, the fig trees appeared on fire escapes and roofs. Papa and Mama nurtured one that grew about four feet tall in a wooden half-barrel.

For several years the fig tree was my bedroom companion from late October to the middle of May. Our apartments did not have central heat. That made a cool bedroom an ideal place to store a fig tree.

Some owners covered their fig tree with a blanket in the fall and kept it in a corridor or in the cellar of the building until spring. The fig trees reminded them of their native Italy where fig trees grew abundantly,

When Papa received his bonus from the government for his military service during World War I, he purchased land in Wilmington, Massachusetts. He built a small cottage there in 1935.

Each spring my bedroom companion traveled to Wilmington where the fig tree was placed on a large, round tree trunk near Papa's vegetable garden.

In the spring, pushcart peddlers with little bells attached to their pushcarts made frequent trips through the streets of Boston's North End. Mama's brother Uncle Jack was one of them.

"Shee-co-ria, scar-oo-la fresca" (fresh escarole, fresh chicory), cried the produce vendors.

"Caudi, caudi" (hot, hot), we heard the crab man call as he toted his steamed crabs down Charter Street.

"How much?" we asked.

"Two centza peese—tree fo fivacentza," he replied. We knew he meant two cents each and three for five cents. We ran to our mothers for change, but didn't always get it.

Papa brought out his wooden bench when spring arrived. He kept it inside all winter near his roll-top desk. Between bakings he sat outside on his bench to enjoy the spring air.

Each new day brought more benches and stools out in front of stores and buildings. Neighbors brought chairs down from their apartments and visited with one another. It happened everyday when it didn't rain.

I knew it was spring.

THE CHILDREN'S GARDENS

In May during the 1930s, when the school bell sounded at the close of school, ten to twenty children gathered outside the Christopher Columbus Elementary School on Tileston Street in Boston's "Little Italy." They waited for Miss Rogers, who walked them to a garden project.

The City of Boston had developed community projects in the early 1900s to benefit children of Spanish, Portuguese, Irish and Italian immigrant families settling into the community. In the 1920s, the Battery Street flower garden flourished under the supervision of Miss Eastwood, a community service employee. Miss Eastwood instructed the children each spring in gardening until Miss Rogers replaced her in the 1930s.

I remember waiting with my third grade classmates after school. Miss Rogers greeted us cheerfully and then led the parade of children toward Battery Street, about two blocks. I followed along for one block and then turned to go home. I never participated in the garden project. I heard about it from some classmates. It wasn't until 1942 that I became reacquainted with what everyone referred to as "Miss Rogers' Garden."

My parents had closed our family bakery on Charter Street in 1941 and reopened a smaller operation on Battery Street in 1942. I developed new friendships there. I remembered some children from middle school days.

When I inquired about the barren lot across from the bakery, Josie, Antoinette and Marshall told me about a garden that had existed there.

"The Boston Harbor Police Station stood at the end of the street next to the garden," Marshall said. He lived in the apartment building next to the bakery. "My two friends Willie Sinopoli and Peter grew flowers there for a few years with Miss Eastwood."

As I listened to my friends, I remembered the smiling, short, plump and motherly Miss Rogers.

"Before she assigned a flower bed," my friends said, "we had to gather all the debris that accumulated during the winder."

"Occasionally, Miss Rogers' sister came as a volunteer helper," Marshall said.

I learned that both ladies taught the children how to turn the soil, plant their marigold, coleus, petunia, pansies, giant sunflowers and morning glory beds. The children nurtured the plants with great pride throughout the summer. Mrs. Rogers showed them how to guide the colorful morning glory vines through the chain-link fence that secured the garden lot. By late July, the giant sunflower plants towered over the little gardeners.

The flower garden became more than a children's project. The neighbors helped to keep it flourishing.

"Mr. Gallo's family lived in the first-floor apartment, next to the garden," Josie recalled. "He attached his water hose to the kitchen faucet and passed it through the window to water the flower beds."

"And Joe the barber (Joe Sinopoli-Willie's father) did the same," Antoinette said. "From his shop, Joe extended his hose across the street and sprayed into the garden."

"We gathered around him on hot days and hollered, spray us, spray us, Joe!" Marshall added.

I visualized the jolly, potbellied, six-foot barber quickly pointing the nozzle upward in the middle of the street, refreshing the children with a cool shower. Joe Sinopoli's barbershop stood two doors away from our bakery.

"Pick the blossoms and give them to your mothers," Miss Rogers told the children. She welcomed their parents to visit and take photographs of the garden.

The stories I heard and photographs I saw greatly expressed the jubilation of the children's participation, not only in this project but also in the second garden project that transported children out of the city.

"My sister Frances and I volunteered ONLY for the vegetable garden," Josie said. "About twenty of us took a bus on Battery Street every Saturday. We rushed to sit close to a window so we could see the beautiful homes, landscaped green lawns, and large trees during our ride to Woburn (about twenty miles north of Boston)."

It became an exciting experience for children who seldom left Boston's North End. They looked forward to being with their instructors, Mr. Crowley and Miss Ferguson, who managed the vegetable garden.

"Each week we were surprised to see the growth of carrots, beets, green peppers, lettuce and tomatoes." Josie said. "We waited to harvest them."

The parents gratefully accepted the fresh vegetables during the Great Depression.

"I'll never forget the warmth of the beet as I pulled it out of the ground," Josie said. "And when my mother cooked it, I couldn't get over how sweet it tasted."

After a pause, she added, "What I enjoyed most about Woburn was when Mr. Crowley took us for a walk in the fields. He taught us the names of the wildflowers we saw. It was so wonderful to breathe the fresh, clean air and walk through the tall grass with the gentle breeze blowing over us."

In August, the gardeners in both projects waited for the annual picnic. It meant another day out of the city.

"I remember asking my mother to wash my 'white ducks' (white slacks) to wear for the outing. I wanted to be with Willie and Peter," Marshall said.

A picnic bus took the children to different places each year. They spent the day swimming at the beaches, playing games or enjoying amusement rides. They waited eagerly for the hot dogs, drinks and ice cream provided by the city's program.

Enthusiasm and excitement filled their hearts when the awards were announced. Antoinette received certificates several years for

best participation in both the flower and vegetable gardens. Josie's
sister, Frances, was also a winner.

"My sister won a pair of roller skates one year for best
vegetables," Josie told me with joy. "She shared them with my
sister Madeleine and me."

They picked more flower blossoms and vegetables from their
gardens. They shared the sunflower seeds with their friends. During
fall and winter days, the children played stick baseball, tin can,
roleevio, jump rope and hopscotch on Battery Street. At times,
they sat on the curbstone in front of Joe Sinopoli's barbershop
or the three long steps of the doorway next to the barbershop
where they huddled together from the cold. They saw the
remaining foliage across the street wither and die. They reminisced
about the hours-spent working in their gardens. Soon, they saw
snowflakes cover their flower garden like a large white blanket.
They stared sadly at the empty white ground and said, "Gee, I
wish it was spring, so we could plant our seeds again."

A young William "Willie" Sinopoli standing beside the tall
sunflower in the garden.

Joseph Sinopoli (Willie's father) a.k.a. "Joe the Barber,"
enjoying a view from he garden.

"Joe the Barber" extended his hose across the street to water the
garden. On hot days he sprayed the children with a cool
shower.

THE CHILDREN'S GARDENS
TREASURED MEMORIES

When our family moved to Battery Street, June 1942, William Sinopoli had already volunteered into the U.S. Army. We met upon his return from Europe in November 1945. We dated and then were married in 1949.

From stories my husband told me and what I heard from my neighbors on Battery Street, I fully understood the impact that the now-empty lot had in their childhood during the Depression years. The delight of being a participant was relayed in their stories.

Today laughs and tears are shared whenever we look at photographs like that of William at nine years old standing proudly near the giant sunflower he had planted; or the one of his father, Joseph Sinopoli sitting on a garden bench among the flower beds. The photograph of William's Dad spraying the children is a favorite of the family.

Vita, Josie (Baudanza) Solimine and Josie (LaGrassa) DiSisto
sitting on the back steps off cottage waiting to go swimming,
Hough's Neck, 1934.

Lucy Orlando, Jennie Pucillo and family digging for clams at
Hough's Neck, 1934. Vita is in the background.

BY THE SEA

My cousins and I cheered when we heard Papa say, "Luciano, how about a picnic at Nahant tomorrow?" In the summer of the 1930s, Papa loved to organize Sunday picnics at the shore. We picnicked at beaches in Revere, Lynn, Nahant, Wollaston, Plymouth, Castle Island, Nantasket, Gloucester, and Ipswich. But Nahant held a special place in my heart.

It seemed like an endless ocean stretched before me when I looked out from the boulders of that Nahant cliff. I felt like I was on top of the world.

Compari Giovanni, Papa's close friend, Uncle Luciano, and Uncle Joe removed empty breadboxes from their delivery vehicles and replaced them with wooden boxes and benches on which the elders could sit.

With permission from Papa, Peter and I sat in one of the delivery trucks with cousins and friends. This allowed our grandmother and Mama's sister to ride in our automobile.

About ten thirty Sunday morning, Mama, our aunts and children arrived carrying hot spaghetti and meatballs, baked chicken, eggplant parmigiana and steamed corn on the cob.*

The elders climbed into the truck and took caution in placing the hot pots away from the young ones. "Be careful with the hot pans," we heard as we sat on the floor and tried to avoid squishing the bread, fruit, or desserts.

---

* See "Tomato Sauce" p. 268
* See "Meatballs" p. 244
* See "Pollo Spezzato Alla Siciliana" p. 254
* See "Eggplant Parmigiana p. 284

"No soda drinks until we get there," we heard as we talked, joked and laughed.

At eleven o'clock, four vehicles carrying twenty-two people and food started out for the ride to Nahant.

The fragrance of food increased our appetites, making the forty-five-minute ride seem like an eternity. Close to noontime, our small convoy traveled up the steep hill to the cliff's parking lot. We could almost hear the people saying, "Here come the Italians!" as we parked. The aroma of the food filtered out of the vehicles along with the passengers. We couldn't wait to eat.

"Remember, you can't go swimming right after you eat." Our mothers warned us as we jumped out to the sandy parking area.

The older children carried out some of the boxes for the elders to sit on. Children sat on the ground to eat the meal. The music from the roller skating rink soon caught our attention. Peter, my cousins, and some of the friends joined in the roller skating. Mama and (grandmother) Nonna marveled, as I did, at how gracefully the couples circled the rink to the music.

Soon I became anxious to roam the boulders of the cliff. A few older cousins agreed to guide the younger children for our search over the boulders. The starfish, hermit crabs and empty shells resting in the tidal pools left by the receded tides became our treasures. Our parents sat on the boulders and watched as we filled our little pails with the periwinkles we snatched from those large rocks.

When we picnicked at Ipswich and other beaches, the men came prepared for clam digging during the low tides. My cousins and I followed them.

"You tell us if any water squirts up at you," the men said. They taught us to look for the tiny openings below our feet, which revealed the hiding places of the clams.

Some Sundays, Papa and friends gathered before sunrise, toting buckets, boots and clamming equipment for a trip to Wollaston Beach. I remember times when Peter and I accompanied them. During those mornings I learned to love the refreshing, quiet early morning atmosphere, the sight of the breathless sunrise, and the feel of my toes squishing into the soft, cool and dark muddy shore. I ignored the foul low tide odor.

Peter and I helped carry the empty buckets along the muddy flats until they became heavy with quahogs, cherry stones, steamers and sea clams.

The most memorable clam-digging experience for me took place during the summer of 1934 along the shores of Hough's Neck, near Quincy and Squantum.

Papa rented a cottage all summer at the water's edge. He told us Mama needed a vacation from her daily bakery activities. During the full moon, the waves from the incoming tide washed up over the first of three steps leading to the cottage porch. My visiting cousins and I enjoyed jumping into the water from the steps during daylight high tides.

During low tides, digging for clams became a daily activity for the children. Our mothers had a perfect view from the cottage porch; but on occasion, they joined us on the flats.

All the catches of the various shellfish that summer became scrumptious meals. Mama and our guests for the day or week prepared them steamed, stuffed, or baked.* We enjoyed some of the cherrystones opened on the shell. Mama used the larger sea clams to make her delicious clam chowder.

Today with each mouthful of shellfish I savor, I relive the glorious moments spent with family by the sea.

---

* See "Linguine with Clams in Bianco" p. 204

Friends on the beach at the North End Park . . . Our community beach and pier on Commercial Street. Photo courtesy of Rose "Dolly" Sorrentino.

A DAY IN THE SUMMER

During hot summer days, weather permitting, I preferred sitting on the wooden bench outside, rather than climbing onto my perch inside. While I waited for friends, I thought about how we often pretended being doctors, nurses or teachers. We included younger cousins, sisters or neighbors to be our patients or students.

Sometimes we played handball up against the red-brick apartment buildings. Or we tried to hit the edge of the sidewalk curb with the ball to have it bounce back to us. If I missed the curb and chased the ball down the street, Mama became angry. She preferred that I stay within her view through the large bakery window.

I waited for companions by drawing a hopscotch game on the sidewalk with chalk. Soon cousin Josie, MaryAnn, Jennie or Nettie joined me.

My brother Peter and friends teased us by hopping in and out of our game, making us angry. Then they decided to mark out the area for a baseball game.

"Why can't you move down the street?" we asked.

Being older, they continued to mark their first base near our hopscotch game and second base on the opposite sidewalk.

"I'm going to tell Mama," we threatened in unison. Some of us had a brother amongst the boys.

That caused a change of heart in the group. They gathered around us and said, "OK, you can all be outfielders."

We happily accepted even though it meant that we had to chase the ball down the hilly street many times.

The thin broom-handle bats and the soft rubber ball kept all of us busy until one boy's swing at the ball sent it through an apartment window. The girls watched the boys run and disappear from sight. They always regrouped at a playground a distance away. Then the street became ours for a game of jump rope, tin can, or hide and seek. Because none of us ever told on the boys, no one received punishment for the broken window.

As the morning progressed, we felt the heat from the sunny day increase. I began to wish for a visit to the North End Park beach along the channel harbor shore.

"Can we go to the park today?" I asked Mama at lunchtime.

"Maybe (aunt) Zia will take you later," she replied.

Mama's sister, Aunt Lena did come about one-thirty, accompanied by her two young children and our Nonna.

We found the park and beach area crowded. Nonna walked down the five or six granite steps to the sandy shore to find us a place to sit. Vita, Nick and I followed Aunt Lena into the bathhouse, to the right of the park grounds. We each paid five cents for a bathing suit that we put on before joining Nonna on the sand.

Already I could feel the hot sun making my skin itch from the navy blue woolen bathing suit. I ran with my cousins down the stairs toward the refreshing water to cool our feet from our short run over the hot cement pavement. Aunt Lena and Nonna walked toward us.

Nonna had removed her shoes and stockings. She always wore ankle-length skirts. She held up her skirt and entered the water up to her ankles.

"Camina, camina" (walk, walk) we called to our grandmother. We waved our hands and asked her to follow us. But she didn't.

"Make a circle and hold hands. "Fa come mia," (Do what I do) Aunt Lena said as she led us a few feet from Nonna.

We laughed joyously as our arms splashed the water over our faces while jumping up and down with my aunt. A while later we returned to the sand.

"Let's cover our legs," I said. The sand and hot sun warmed our bodies.

Through the noisy crowd, we became aware of screams from people in the water. I suddenly realized that boys were pushing girls off the large raft into the water. Others dove from the pier's pilings. The double-decker pier stretched out horizontally before us about eighty feet from the shoreline. Some daring swimmers even climbed up onto the canopy that shaded one end of the second deck of the pier. Butterflies fluttered in my stomach. To me it seemed like they jumped a mile's distance into the water from the canopy that everyone called "the shed." I held my breath and waited to hear loud cheers. Then I knew the diver had safely returned to the surface.

We needed something to do after playing in the sand awhile. I thought about the sprinkler. Being ten, five years older than Cousin Vita, I asked my aunt, "Can we go up to the sprinkler and wash off the sand?"

She even agreed to have three-year-old Nickie come with us. Then I saw Nonna and my aunt move to sit on the granite steps closer to us. They sat with their feet in the water of the high tide that covered three or four of the granite steps. They could see us running in and out from under the sprinkler. How wonderful it felt to have the cold water remove the sand from our arms and legs. It relieved the itch from the woolen bathing suits.

"Vita, dovemo andare ora." (We have to leave now). They both called out to us.

It seemed too brief a stay. We didn't want to acknowledge hearing them. We continued running back and forth from the sprinkler until they came real close. Then we followed them into the bathhouse.

I couldn't wait to take off that scratchy bathing suit. Aunt Lena paid one cent extra for each of us to have a small bar of soap and a towel for our shower. Vita and I showered together while Nick showered with his mother.

I loved having the warm water cascading over my body.

"Don't you wish we all had showers at home?" I asked Vita.

She looked a little bewildered. Like me she had never seen a shower in the apartment buildings. We took baths in the large galvanized metal tub in our kitchen. Our hot water came from the copper water tank, heated by lighting the gas burner attached to it. Sometimes Mama and Aunt Lena took us for showers on Ladies' Day at the North Bennet Street bathhouse.

"Presto," (hurry) Aunt Lena called to us. "E tempo di lasciare" (It's time to leave).

"Can Vita have supper with us?" I asked my aunt during our return to the bakery.

Aunt Lena often returned in the evening. The air in the apartments remained stagnant even with windows ajar.

"Lassila cha." (Leave her here). Mama said. "Torna sta sera." (Come back tonight).

Vita and I smiled approvingly. "When your mother comes back later, maybe she'll take us to the park again."

A SUMMER EVENING

After supper, Cousin Vita and I sat on the bench outside the bakery and waited for her mother and our grandmother to join us.

Vita and I watched as the neighbors came with their stools, chairs and benches. They slowly filled the sidewalks on both sides of the street, leaving little room for walking. On Friday and Saturday evenings, our street resembled a block party.

"Lucia, I think I'll take them for a walk to the park," Aunt Lena told Mama when she arrived.

My cousins and I ran through the narrow alley next to the bakery and across the small vacant lot to Foster Street. We waited at the end of that short street for my aunt and grandmother to lead us to the park entrance across the busy Commercial Street. We saw some boys with gloves and bats waiting to play a game of baseball. Vita, Nick and I held hands and ran left across the ball field toward the entrance to the pier. We stopped at the bocce area briefly to watch one man roll out his gray hard ball on the bocce court toward the scoring ball. We held our breath as his ball passed three other balls. Then we cheered with the crowd as the gray ball stopped closest to the black ball and scored a point.

When Nonna and Aunt Lena caught up to us, we walked up the ramp onto the lower pier. A light, refreshing breeze blew around us. I noticed Nonna pulling her light shawl over her shoulders.

As we approached the stairs leading to the upper deck, I remembered hearing Peter and his friends saying, "All the boys take their dates to the second deck. Everybody knows it's a lovers' lane." I wanted to see who was up there, but Aunt Lena insisted on keeping us on the lower deck.

"Let's see if we can see jelly fish from here," I said as I looked down over the black metal railing into the dark green water. "No jelly fish and no one diving from the pier."

Cousins Nick and Vita peered through the railing bars. "Look! Kids are jumping from the raft," they cried. Then I saw them cup their hands over their noses, disliking the low tide odor.

We watched some swimmers return to the shore. I loved following the waves rolling out from under the pier and breaking into white foam before sliding onto the sandy beach.

"Camminamo, ragazzi" (Let's walk, children). Nonna called out.

We walked toward the end of the pier where Nonna and Aunt Lena finally found a place to sit. I took my cousins to the opposite railing.

"Look at the ships at the Charlestown Navy Yard," I said pointing.

I wanted them to see the destroyers and the *Constitution* docked across the water. "And there's the ferry we take when we go to see Uncle Jimmy.

"I see it," Vita cried out. "See it, Nick, over there?"

Dusk approached slowly. Soon lights became visible from the ships in the navy yard. Before long we saw the orange-crimson sun spread its beautiful hues over the sky and harbor waters. We watched until it disappeared from the horizon, over the Charles River.

"I like watching the stars," Vita said. Stars became visible in the darkening blue sky. They blended with the twinkling lights of the ships in the navy yard. We saw very little sky or stars from our apartment windows or from the street because of the lights and tall apartment buildings.

"Vinemmo domani," Mama (Can we come back tomorrow, Mama)? Vita called to her mother who approached us.

"Viremmo" (We'll see), her mother replied. "E tempo di lasciare ora" (It's time to leave now).

I noticed that softer voices replaced the loud chatter on the pier as the sky continued to darken. The pier seemed peaceful, and the air so refreshing as we walked toward the exiting ramp.

On our return to the hot, crowded Charter Street we greeted Mama's two brothers and their wives sitting in front of the bakery. I saw my brother Peter and friends with some of my girl cousins sitting across the street enjoying their ice cream.

Guess we missed the ice cream man, I thought. He regularly pushed his cart through the neighborhood streets in the summer. A while later, we heard the crab man hollering, "caudi caudi,"(hot, hot). We begged our parents to purchase some periwinkles for one cent a cup, or some steamed crabs for two cents apiece.

The children got periwinkles to share, while the adults bought some crabs. Peter and the teenagers bought a few crabs and returned to sit across the street. Mama passed out some safety pins that we used to pry out the tiny periwinkle from its shell so we could eat it.

We tossed the crab and periwinkle shells onto the street from our curbstone seats. It amused us to hear the crushing sound of shells when an automobile, pushcart vendor, or horse-drawn wagon passed over them. It frightened me, though, when I saw a horse struggle over the slippery shells. Poor animal I thought.

"Here come the sweepers," I heard Papa say later.

We watched as the men of the Works Project Administration swept the streets. They gathered everything into neat piles with their long-handled brushes. The stench of crab and periwinkle shells filled the air. A truck followed with more workers who tossed the debris into the back of the city truck.

"The water truck is coming! Let's move before we get wet," I told Vita, as I heard the spraying of water. As the truck turned onto Charter Street from Salem Street, neighbors rushed to return to their apartments with their stools and chairs. Papa took our bench into the bakery. The time had arrived to say "Good night."

As I lay in my bed that evening remembering the activities of the day, I heard the voices of young and older men through our open apartment windows. They remained outside late on weekend evenings. They gathered in front of poolrooms or stores that they rented as a clubhouse. The background of laughter and people conversing outside kept me awake. I began thinking about what to do the next day. Soon the conversations ceased and the sweet harmonizing voices accompanied by a harmonica flowed into my bedroom. The soothing mellow sounds of songs like "That Old Gang of Mine" lulled me to sleep.

CARNEVALE

Carnevale, like Mardi Gras, begins a three-day celebration before Ash Wednesday. In our home, the tradition brought from "the old country" was to have relatives gather for the noon meal on Carnevale Sunday. We woke up that morning to the sizzling of meatballs* frying on the stove. It blended with the scent of simmering onions and tomatoes from another pot. We enjoyed one or two of Mama's hot meatballs for breakfast while we listened to recordings of Enrico Caruso and others on the Italian Radio Hour.

My parents had a collection of recordings by Italian and American performers. When we didn't listen to the radio, Papa let me wind up the Victrola to listen to Nicola Paone's Italian skits that always brought tears of laughter. Papa often listened to the recording of Paul Whitman's orchestra playing "Japanese Sandman" or of Al Jolson singing "Rock-a-bye My Baby with a Gypsy Melody

During church services that morning, the priest reminded us of the rules of the Lenten fast to begin on Ash Wednesday. But my thoughts focused on the festivities forthcoming that evening.

Returning from St. Anthony's Church, our nostrils detected the aromas of a variety of sauces and meats cooking in the different apartments we passed. We're not the only ones to have guests for dinner, I thought.

On Carnevale Sunday, our parents invited Nonna, Mama's brother Jack and family, Aunt Lena and family, and Uncle Sam

---

* See "Meatballs" p. 244

for noontime dinner. Nonna and Aunt Lena arrived earlier to help Mama make homemade Linguine. My cousins and I watched Nonna knead the dough that Aunt Lena and Aunt Martha waited to roll into thin, large round sheets. To keep us away from their work, Nonna gave the children a piece of dough to play with.

Mama sprinkled each round sheet with some flour. Then she folded it into a long portion about three inches in width. With a sharp knife, she cut it into narrow strips that she called linguine.

As Mama cut the folded dough, Aunt Lena gently picked up the linguine and rested it on a floured tablecloth on Mama's bed. Meanwhile we saw the large pot of water being heated on the stove. By the time the women finished their work, the pot boiled. A few minutes later, we all sat at the table for Sunday dinner.

Papa and Uncle Luciano, Mama's brother, were both self-taught mandolin players. They occasionally entertained us after dinner, especially on Carnevale Sunday. Uncle Luciano and family joined us from their first-floor apartment below us. We all enjoyed singing the old songs that they played.

When we saw Mama prepare coffee to be served later, we knew that our departure time was nearing. Like my cousins, I waited anxiously all day to dress in my Sunday best for the festivities we planned to attend.

"Please, Mama, curl our hair," I pleaded

I watched her hold the curling iron over the gas stove burner until it heated enough to create the waves my cousins and I wanted. We prayed for the curls to last through the night.

A few days before Carnevale Sunday, Uncle Luciano and the social committee prepared for the festivities to take place in the their social club. We referred to it as "La Sala" (the hall). The large, old corner building with a curved facade stood at the corner of Hanover and Charter Street. It is now the site of the District #1 Fire Station. A coffee shop and a large hardware store occupied the street-floor area. We entered from Charter Street and climbed the stairs to the first floor to enter the hall. The steep, narrow stairway creaked with age. The members of La Societa Salemitana, all immigrant families from Salemi, Sicily, enjoyed having a place for meetings and family gatherings.

The doors of the hall opened Carnevale Sunday at seven that evening for the festivities. Children of all ages accompanied their parents.

Uncle Luciano helped sell pizza and soft drinks. The five-cent pieces sold out quickly. Mothers with young children came with fruit and snacks. We snickered at seeing some mothers modestly breast-feeding babies at the rear of the hall. Before the music began, we ran around the large hall, greeting our friends. We enjoyed sliding on the smooth dance floor, but the elders kept reprimanding us.

My cousins and I watched the musicians prepare their sheet music on the small stage. We listened with hands cupped over our ears while the musicians went through their warm ups and tune-ups on a saxophone, clarinet, guitar, piano and accordion.

We hastily ran to our parents when Don Pasquale, our local barber and the Societa President, lined up the committee members. We knew he was about to begin the festivities. He signaled to the musicians to play "La Marcia Reale" (Italian National Anthem). The committee marched around the hall. After a brief welcoming speech with a wave of his arm in the air, Don Pasquale called out, "Musica" (music). The music began, the dance floor shook, and the walls vibrated to the polkas, waltzes, fox trots and mazurkas they played.

Children joined the adults on the dance floor. That is where my brother Peter and Cousin Josie, Uncle Luciano's daughter, taught me how to dance. I was six or seven, thin and small. I felt like I was flying when they twirled me around on the slippery floor. I never lost the love for a fast mazurka or polka.

The festivities took place on three evenings, lasting until eleven each evening. The second most exciting time was the third night when several members and their families arrived in costume. We waited especially to see our neighbor enter as Marie Antoinette. One hand clutched the sparkling handle of her elaborate mask that covered her eyes and face. The other held the colorful silk shawl that graced her shoulders over her gorgeous gown. We watched the beautifully masqueraded couple walk elegantly through the crowd.

I remember another family arriving jubilantly in farmer's attire and masked faces. They tossed tangerines with their Scaletta into the gathering. The mechanism came from Italy. It consisted of narrow wooden slats joined so they could spread, like an accordion, as the carrier pressed a lever. The tangerine secured to the top slat propelled into the crowd. The older children scrambled to catch a tangerine. This frightened young children like myself. Shortly after their entrance, the music began and couples returned to dancing.

"A ballamu." (Let's dance.) Papa said to me.

He conversed with those in costume as we danced. My fear subsided.

During that evening, the committee members voted for the first, second, and third prize winners. Later, Don Pasquale called everyone to attention to announce the winners. The clapping and cheering filled the hall. The costumed winners removed their masks as they approached Don Pasquale for their gift. They received a monetary gift, a few pounds of pork sausage, or a piglet for Easter dinner. Once again, Don Pasquale called for "Musica." The musicians played, and people danced until closing time.

After three evenings of music and dancing, I felt both tired and sad. The thought of returning for one more evening of celebration allowed me to wait patiently through the forty days of Lent. I looked forward to returning Easter evening to La Sala for the conclusion of the holiday festivities.

LENT

During the Depression, servings of meatless meals increased in our home in observance of the Lenten fast. Mama had learned during bleak years in her homeland how to prepare healthy economical meals by substituting vegetables or legumes for meat. We enjoyed pasta with escarole, ricotta (Italian cream cheese), broccoli, cauliflower, lentil soup, pea soup, or white or red kidney beans. At times she served pasta with fried eggs in tomato sauce, peas in tomato sauce, or boiled artichoke pieces in tomato sauce flavored with garlic, basil and olive oil.*

From Ash Wednesday to Easter Sunday, days passed slowly. The only excitement was seeing Mama going through bureau draws and closets, removing clothing that no longer fit Peter and me.

An exchange of hand-me-downs took place during Lent within the families of nearby relatives and friends. Needy families in our community greatly appreciated receiving hand-me-downs. Lack of income made it difficult for parents to purchase children's clothing for a holiday like Easter.

Mama loved to sew, as did many of her friends in our neighborhood. She planned to make a new dress for me each Easter. She looked through the advertisements of dresses in the newspapers for something that pleased her, or she purchased a pattern she liked in Joe Shuman's store.

Most often, when she found a dress she liked in the newspaper, she cut out her version of the pattern from brown paper or

---

* See " Pasta Con Broccoli" p. 292
* See "Lentil Soup" p. 287
* See "Spit Green Pea Soup" p. 298

newspaper. She held the individual pieces of her cut pattern up against my body to make size corrections. She diligently sewed the dress on her Singer pedal sewing machine in our apartment during evenings. It amazed me how close she came to the advertised dress.

Mama shopped separately for clothing for Peter and me. I waited for the day we went shopping for new shoes and a hat. My last year's hat went to a needy family. The thought of the new items to wear Easter morning brightened the remaining Lenten days for me.

A three tier alter dedicated to honor St. Joseph. Celebrations
took place in the homes of many paesani. This is a celebration
in the home of the Leonardo Liuzza family.
(Photo courtesy of Mary Ann (Liuzza) Tucceri)

ST. JOSEPH'S DAY CELEBRATION
IN THE HOME

"He's going to build 'La Cena' (the table and altar) for Sunday," Peter said.

We watched our great Uncle Nino carry a few boards to his fourth-floor apartment. "Is Sunday St. Joseph's Day?" I asked.

"No, but he always has the celebration the closest Sunday to March nineteen," he replied.

Papa had told us about his maternal uncle whom we called Zio (Zee-o) Nino and his wife Zia (Zee-a) Marianna. They had come to Boston from Sicily in the early 1900s. Papa lived with them when he arrived in 1907. Zio worked for the railroad. He and his wife raised six children. During a difficult time in her life, Zia (aunt) had prayed to Saint Joseph for his intercession.

In thanksgiving for graces received, Papa said she vowed to feed many people in her home for the remainder of her life on the Feast Day of St. Joseph. During confusing days of being in America, she felt his help.

Zio Nino and his family lived in the apartment building above our bakery. Their married daughter, Marion, her husband and three children lived in the same building.

In preparation for the celebration, Zio Nino removed furniture from one room of their apartment. In it he built a temporary three-tired altar with an open frame around the altar. Then he placed a rectangular table in front of the altar. He saved and used the same boards each year for this project.

"Is Zio Nino going to invite the same kids to sit at La Cena?" I asked Mama. "We'll see," she replied.

Before the celebration day, our great uncle and his wife

decided whom to invite to represent the Holy Family at their Saint Joseph Feast. A teenage boy, a teenage girl, and a younger child (not necessarily from one family) were chosen from the neighborhood. The parents of each child felt privileged in having the child chosen.

An evening before the celebration, Mama and I went to Zio's apartment. We found several paesane (hometown lady friends) watching one of the women mixing and kneading a large amount of dough. Like Mama, the women came each year voluntarily to make the many dozens of little breads for this St. Joseph Celebration.

I sat near Mama engrossed in watching four women sitting on four sides of the large, square, wooden lapboard on which they shaped small portions of dough into miniature breads. While one made little round breads covered with sesame seeds, another rolled dough and joined the two ends. She snipped the edges and added whole cloves to represent the crown of thorns. There were enough helpers there to alternate at the wooden lapboard in order to create miniature scalas (ladders), staffs, birds, angels, hammers and scissors. It fascinated me. All the bread shapes had some significance to the Holy Family. Each little loaf received a gentle egg wash before being baked in Zia Marianna's stove oven.

Later that week, Peter and I saw Zio Nino and two (family friends) arrive in an automobile. We watched the men fill their arms with evergreens stored in the trunk and back seat of the car. As they entered the apartment building beside us, the smell of freshly cut leaves lingered in the air.

"Where do they get those?" I asked Peter.

"They go to the fields owned by these friends," Peter said. "The men allow Zio Nino to take some every year."

I waited Friday evening for Mama to say, "Let's go upstairs, Vita." I wanted to see the altar and fixings.

I felt like we had walked into an orange grove as we entered the apartment. We walked through the large kitchen and saw the wooden frame in the bedroom covered with green leaves. We greeted some of the ladies and their children who had been with us earlier in the week. Papa's brother Joe, his wife and two girls were there among the children close to our age. Everyone was busy working and conversing. While Cousin Vita (Uncle Nino's daughter) stood in the kitchen ironing linens for the altar, I joined my young cousins watching the women in the altar room. We mingled among the ladies but they preferred that we stay in the kitchen while they tied oranges and tangerines to the frame. Others began tying the little breads, adding them to the frame among the oranges and tangerines.

When they completed that project, Zia Marianna placed the ironed linens on the altar shelves and altar table. In the kitchen some ladies began washing and drying dishes and utensils needed on Sunday.

The next morning, as I sat on my perch in the bakery, I saw Zio Nino enter with three large loaves of bread to be baked. His daughter Anna later told me the long loaf I saw represented the lily, the symbol of purity of the Blessed Mother; the staff-shaped loaf represented Saint Joseph; and the large round doughnut-shaped loaf represented the crown of light or halo of the Infant Jesus. The top of each loaf was decorated with tiny pieces of dough.

I watched Papa and Zio Nino add some sesame seeds to the loaves and then brush each loaf with egg wash. I know that Zio said a silent prayer as Papa slipped the breads into the oven.

How beautiful the large golden-topped loaves looked that evening, resting on the altar shelves. Shinning green leaves, dotted with oranges, tangerines and miniature breads framed the shelves and table.

Zia brought out her colorful photograph of the Holy Family to be placed on the altar shelf. Cousin Vita put white candles and a small vase of flowers on each side of the photo. A bowl of fruit and some empty wine bottles also rested on the altar, the same wine bottles that Zia Marianna used each year.

"We wait for the priest, now," someone said.

He arrived later to bless La Cena.

"Don't remove these," I heard Zia say as we prepared to leave. She had placed a bowl with oranges on her hutch.

"What's that bowl for?" I asked Mama.

"The children who sit at the table representing the Holy Family will have to wash their hands in this special bowl of water. It's a blessing of the hands."

It did confuse me, but I accepted her explanation.

On Sunday morning, we found our thin, silver-haired Zia frying artichoke slices that had been dipped in beaten eggs and coated with bread crumbs. The aroma of fried smelts blended with stuffed artichokes simmering on the stove. Meanwhile, her two younger daughters, Josie and Anna scrubbed pots and pans at the kitchen sink. Some of Zia Marianna's friends had already arrived with their husbands and children. Her brother Paul and family and our Uncle Joe (Papa's brother) and family joined us. Mama helped as the ladies cut off the outer crust from a number of loaves of bread. They placed the soft white insides of the loaves in a large ceramic bowl.

"How much parsley?" Cousin Marion asked.

Two ladies measured and spread parsley and sugar over the bread. Then Zia Marianna added olive oil and tossed the mixture gently before setting it aside.

My mouth watered. I desperately wanted to taste this bread mixture. But we all knew that we had a very long wait for the traditional "pasta culla muddica" (spaghetti with bread crumbs). Mama called it the poor man's meal.

The three special children invited to portray the Holy Family arrived about eleven thirty that morning dressed in their very best Sunday clothes. We knew that Zio Nino wanted to start the serving at noon.

"Carry each serving to Zio who will offer it first to the Holy Family," Cousin Marion told us. She was Zio Nino's oldest child who had children of her own waiting to serve. Everyone waited until the "Holy Family" members completed their meal.

Zia Marianna had decided from the first day of her vow that there would be no meat served on that day of celebration.

Zio Nino stood at the altar table beside the "Holy Family." He looked so distinguished in his white shirt and tie. Like myself, the children were very eager to hand him our plate of food. We stepped aside as he served it to one of the children.

"Viva, San Giuseppe, Viva!" (Hail, St Joseph, Hail!) Zio cried out occasionally. The adults loudly replied the same.

The three Holy Family children seated at La Cena had been told that they had to taste everything that was served to them, but they did not necessarily have to eat the entire portion. We waited for Zio Nino to give us a dish to return to the kitchen. With each serving, we became more anxious to taste the foods we diligently carried to Zio Nino. We also waited for him to grant us permission, on our return to the kitchen, to eat a portion of what had not been touched by one of his special guests. That became our big treat.

Zio Nino sliced one of the large round loaves from the altar as the children requested bread for their meal. Portions of fried smelts, fried baccala, breaded and fried cauliflower, stuffed peppers and various vegetable omelets were served along with a serving of the traditional spaghetti with bread crumbs. Their meal ended with fruit, nuts and dessert. Zio Nino thanked his three special young guests for participating that day. Then they departed with some of the breads.

As the "Holy Family" departed, we waited anxiously for the very large pot of water on the stove to boil. When it did, Zia cooked the spaghetti for our meal. Meanwhile people hustled and bustled in the kitchen, cleaning and putting away items no longer needed. The remaining foods were placed in serving platters and rested covered on the stovetop and in the oven to be served later.

There was talk and laughter, and some scolding of young children waiting impatiently for dinner. The men began to move chairs into the altar room for seating.

I watched as Zia stirred the eight or ten pounds of spaghetti that one of the ladies gently dropped into the boiling pot. The twenty-five or thirty people, young and old, waited eagerly to gather at the large round kitchen table where Zia would serve the spaghetti.

After draining the pasta, Zia Marianna tossed the cooked spaghetti onto the clean wooden lapboard now resting on her kitchen table. Cousin Marion and several of the women spread the prepared bread crumbs over this huge mound while Zia mixed the bread crumbs into the pasta.

A loud "Viva San Giuseppe, Viva" by Zio Nino signaled the start of our dinner.

After enjoying la pasta culla mudica (the pasta with the bread crumbs), I waited for neighbors and visitors to come to view La Cena (the altar and table). Many visited briefly while others lingered either in the kitchen or in the altar room. Our older cousins served coffee and cookies to the visitors. The custom was to take home, if desired, one of the little breads, or a tangerine or orange decorating La Cena.

Everyone waited for the gentlemen to arrive to recite Sicilian verses about St. Joseph. I learned about my ancestors' deep devotion to this Saint and about the origin of the feast. Some told about the various graces received by friends and families of their hometown. In closing, each speaker expressed gratitude at being allowed to recite that day. Each ended on a humorous note, pleading to Zio Nino for a refreshing beverage at the close of his ten-minute narration.

"Viva, San Giuseppe, Viva," we heard as the gentleman accepted the glass of Zio Nino's homemade wine. Everyone replied, "Viva, San Giuseppe, Viva."

The day's events made the time pass quickly. Other paesani in the North End had the same celebration on that same day but often times we only stayed at Zio Nino's home. Mama noticed that Peter and I were ready for bed by nine o'clock. Though sad when we departed, I anticipated being at another St. Joseph celebration at Zio's home next year.

Jerry DeRosa's Butcher shop during holy week. Butcher shops displayed traditional whole lambs, piglets, goats and rabbits that were bought by patrons for their Easter Dinner. (Photo courtesy of Rose Sinopoli)

Peter's and Lucy's display of "Cannatone" in Orlando's Bakery during Holy Week 1950s.

Vita preparing Cannatone for baking in her Cape Cod home.

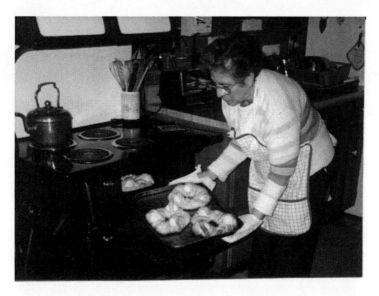

Vita removing baked Cannatone from her oven. (1995)

HOLY WEEK

We thought of the palms received on Palm Sunday as a gift. Children like receiving gifts, but our parents taught us to share our palms. When we left church, we exchanged one stem each with our parents. Mama and Papa exchanged palms with a friend or relative we met.

At home, Papa showed us how he shaped a few palms into a cross. We watched him braid the palms and make a cross out of it. Each of us pinned one to a coat or jacket for the day. Papa kept one in his automobile.

After dinner, we visited Nonna to give her our palm. We watched the aunts and uncles, also visiting, as they crimped and folded palms until each of us had another keepsake of our own. I saved mine from year to year.

Our community took on an unmistakable appearance of Little Italy that week. The main event on Holy Thursday was visiting the churches. With four Catholic churches in the North End, the streets became crowded with residents and suburban visitors all day. People visited churches, also browsed through the streets, stopped for lunch or suppers while others stopped at a coffee shop for a piece of Italian pastry. Many came to purchase specialty items from bakeries, fish markets, butchers, or produce vendors for the holiday.

The North End pastry shops baked marzipan-type lambs (sugar figurines) of all sizes. They displayed their pastel-colored marzipan creations in their windows that drew many onlookers into their shops. Each day on our way home from school, we looked into the windows and dreamed of receiving one for Easter. Mostly though, we found the less-expensive Zeppoli di San

Giuseppe at our table. This pastry, shaped like a doughnut, filled with yellow cream, and covered with a thin glaze, became a traditional specialty at Easter. St. Joseph's Day, celebrated on March 19, was always during Lent and close to Holy Thursday.

The butcher shops displayed, among their other meat products, traditional whole lambs, piglets, goats and rabbits. Families purchased them live to prepare later for Sunday dinner.

"I've got my lucky rabbit's foot!" we heard on our way to school. "The butcher gave it to my mother."

It was the thing to have as a youngster. A dry, cleaned rabbit's foot or tail became our lucky charm that we carried in our coat or jacket pocket.

The Italians who lived in villages in Italy had to travel a distance from their homes to tend to their large gardens. The men hunted rabbits for food. Their wives learned to prepare delicious meals with the meat. They dried the rabbit fur in the sun. The women used the fur to decorate hats and coat collars. When they migrated to America, they asked their butcher to supply rabbits for a holiday meal. Many continued to dry the fur that they used for decorating clothing.

My parents spoke often of their chores as children in Italy. They told us how they helped in raising pigs, lambs and goats. Few families had enough land to raise cows, so they raised goats for their milk.

For special holiday meals, Mama said her father sacrificed one of their lambs, piglets, or a young goat for their holiday meal. Sometimes he bartered with a brother, uncle or neighbor, offering grain, olive oil or services in exchange for holiday meat.

On Holy Week in the North End, I accompanied Mama to the fish market. I saw the dried salted cod (baccala) and dried salted haddock (pesce stocco) soaking in water. While Mama made purchases in the busy Giuffre's Fish Market on Salem Street, I watched the snails climbing up the side of a wooden barrel. The barrel rested on the wide doorstep of the store's entrance. Sometimes Mama purchased escargot and prepared it as her mother had done in Salemi, Sicily. Escargot was available along the coastal shores of Sicily. People enjoyed them prepared with garlic and tomato. Mama added chopped, Sicilian, long green squash (cucuzza) to the mixture. Cucuzza is similar to zucchini in texture but lighter in color with a sweeter flavor. During Holy Week, the bakeries displayed tarralli, one dozen on a string, in their doorways or windows. They come flavored with fennel seeds, or ground black pepper, or poppy seeds. These round little loaves, shaped like bagels, become hard when baked. Tarralli are great for dunking in coffee or tea. Most men enjoyed them dunked in wine.

The immigrants found chickens inexpensive and available in America during the Depression. Mama told me that almost every family in her Italian village raised chickens, hens and roosters.

"That's how we got our eggs," she said. "Sometimes we cooked a chicken as a special meal, like on Christmas Day. We mostly ate vegetables and beans."

I remember walking with my mother weekly to a chicken store on Commercial Street (at the end of Charter Street). Feathers and sawdust covered the wooden floor. We mingled with Jewish customers. Some families still lived in the North End. Others came from the West End and the suburbs. A Rabbi was present in the store for those who came to purchase a kosher chicken and eggs.

It's difficult to forget the cackling chickens housed in wooden crates, stacked almost to the ceiling. Mama took her time selecting the chicken size she wanted. Feathers flew out of the crates each time the crate door opened. The steam from the back room, the wet feathers, and the sawdust odors choked me. I couldn't wait to leave. Mama made her final choice, and we joined those in line. I watched with sadness as the clerk added Mama's choice to the number of chickens with tied legs hanging from hooks. I was uncomfortable seeing the worker pull or sever their necks. They fluttered wildly for a few minutes before hanging still. I wished for Mama to take the chicken home alive as others did so I wouldn't have to experience that scene. We waited for the workers to dunk the chicken in the hot water. We watched them pluck the feathers and clean it for us.

On Wednesday evening of Holy Week, Mama boiled several dozen eggs for the "Cannatone" (Easter Breads).* Though known as Easter Breads, Papa mixed cake-like dough. My parents knew that a number of people began their Easter food shopping on Holy Thursday. That afternoon Mama and Papa rolled and braided the special dough for the Cannatone. I watched Mama place the hard-boiled eggs between the braids of each loaf. She rolled narrow pieces of dough and placed them crisscross over the egg, securing it in the braid. They made different-size loaves — some with two, three, or four eggs.

While they baked, Mama mixed her icing for the Easter Breads. Sometimes I helped sprinkle the nonpareils over the icing. After baking, Mama placed some in the display window for sale. I saw her place a dozen or so with one egg on a shelf.

"Which one is for me?"

Invariably we ate one that evening after supper. We expected to have another one on Easter morning.

---

* See "Cannatone" p. 310

THE VISITATIONS

After school on Holy Thursday, Mama reminded me "Un vari lontano." (Don't go far.)

I knew we had to visit the churches. Peter, being older, went with his friends while we waited for Nonna, Aunt Lena and the cousins. First we walked to St. Stephen's Church on Hanover Street and then to St. Anthony's Church on Prince Street. Sometimes we left Nonna in church to say her rosary with the Franciscan Third Order women. We walked on to St. Mary's Church on Endicott Street.

The long waiting lines moved slowly in and out of the churches. The fragrance from the fresh flower displays on the altars together with that of lit candles greeted us at each entrance. We admired the beautifully decorated altars. We knelt in a pew to say a prayer or stopped to light a candle before exiting.

After our visit at St. Mary's Church we returned to meet Nonna. We walked together to Sacred Heart's Church at North Square, near Paul Revere house. Though the custom was for Catholics to visit three, five, or seven churches that day, we usually visited the four churches in the North End community. When Holy Thursday took place in April, and we enjoyed some spring-like weather, it was inevitable that we would stop to talk with many friends, relatives and neighbors. People lingered in the streets as we made our way through the North End for the visitations. In later years as a teenager, I preferred to walk with my friends. The long waiting line to enter each church gave us a chance to mingle with school friends and people we did not see often during the winter months. When weather permitted, we extended our walk to a fifth church — St. Joseph's Church in the West End. It became an evening of visitations, prayer and time with friends.

It was difficult during the depression years to be excited about new clothes for Easter. Most homes couldn't afford them. But as we got older, and we became employed, enthusiasm for the coming holiday increased as we exchanged comments about our intended outfits for the holiday. All the pastry shops and coffee shops remained open until late. We stopped in one to talk further about our Easter outfit while we enjoyed our coffee. A group of us sometimes ended the evening at a friend's house before returning home. The streets remained crowded until late evening on Holy Thursday.

HOLY SATURDAY

On Holy Saturday morning, Mama handed Peter a small empty bottle. "Peter, take your sister with you to church to get L'aqua Santa (Holy Water)."

That kept us out of the bakery for at least two hours.

We met our friends waiting in line for the priest to fill our bottle. Mama used the Holy Water to sprinkle a little throughout the bakery each year as she recited a short prayer. Later she repeated that in our apartment.

The aura of a holiday was present as the hustle and bustle of a Saturday in the bakery doubled. Everyone moved at a faster pace. Papa hired neighborhood teenagers to help when the workload increased. They prepared and stacked breadboxes, carried flour bags from the stockpile to the mixer and delivered various sandwich loaves to several neighborhood sandwich shops. I helped Peter carry the large breadbasket at noontime to Red's Sandwich Shop on Foster Street (one street away). Hungry customers' eyes lit up when we walked in with the freshly baked "spuckies" (submarine shaped loaves) for their sandwiches.

When the bakery helpers completed their work, Papa paid them and gave each one a large loaf of bread for their family.

"Lucia, salvami due pane," (Lucy, save me two breads), Aunt Martha called out from the doorway.

She was not alone that day in calling out a bread order to Mama. She knew what her customers purchased. As she received the orders, she jotted down notes and stored the loaves on the shelves behind her.

Later in the afternoon, I watched from my perch as Mama

and Aunt Lena prepared the ricotta pies (Italian cream cheese pies).* They baked them in the oven,

Then they mixed dough by hand for cannoli shells. They rolled each shell individually and deep-fried them on the small gas burner available in the workshop. As I watched them roll out the cannoli, I could almost taste the ricotta filling. Sometimes Mama cooked up a batch of yellow cream also to use as an alternate filling. I liked either filling, but I knew I had to wait until after Sunday dinner to eat one.*

People entered and exited the store all day. Papa and Mama had little time to sit. We ate our meals hastily.

The drivers returned from their suburban bread deliveries around supper time. Papa counted out what loaves remained for sale. He put aside two loaves for our home. Many times, the bread sold out completely, including the loaves Papa saved for us. It was not unusual for us to have yesterday's bread for our table.

The times when bread remained in the display window into late evening before a holiday, Papa made a decision around 9:30 pm. . Peter and I knew he planned to make a delivery. We helped store the loaves in cardboard boxes. We accompanied Papa to the Home for Little Wanderers and the Home for Italian Orphaned Children, both in Jamaica Plain. They gratefully accepted the donations.

We felt good all the way home and ready for the Easter Holiday.

---

* See "Ricotta Cheese Pie" p. 320
* See "Cannoli p.312

EASTER

The Old North Church bells rang out familiar Sunday hymns heard throughout the neighborhood. It alerted me to Easter morning. At last I could wear my new dress, hat and shoes. Mama placed Easter Bread* on the table for each of us and a bowl of hard-boiled eggs.

"After Mass, we're going to Uncle Joe's," Papa said at breakfast.

I preferred to return home, as I knew my cousins would be coming. But Papa's traditional visits brought us to Uncle Joe's home after church services. Then we visited a short time with Papa's only other relatives in America, Uncle Nino and family. Uncle Joe worked for Papa. Uncle Nino and family lived above the bakery. It seemed foolish to Peter and me to visit that morning since we saw them almost everyday. We watched the clock for departing time. We knew Mama planned to serve dinner shortly after noon. Aunt Lena and Nonna had arrived as Papa, Peter and me departed for church. They came to help Mama make the ravioli for dinner. I knew the Easter meal would keep us at the table, eating for a long time that day.

We completed our visits with Papa and returned home. A few minutes later, Uncle Sammy and Uncle Frank, Aunt Lena's husband, arrived with a box of Italian pastry, purchased at our favorite pastry shop—Mondello's on Hanover Street.

We took our seats at the large round kitchen table. Nonna served us a small portion of Acine-de-Pepe (pasta) and a few miniature meatballs with the homemade chicken soup. She knew

---

* See "Cannatone" p.310

we wanted the ravioli but consoled us with "Un dicchia"(Just a little).

We waited patiently for Mama to serve her large platter of ricotta-filled ravioli with sauce. Aunt Lena placed a large bowl of meatballs next to the ravioli platter. It always amazed me at the quantity of ravioli the women had made.

Mama taught us to remain at the table until we tasted a portion of the roasted lamb leg* and potatoes garnished with parsley and garlic. She served that after the ravioli. Peter and I waited for the fried wild mushrooms to eat with the lamb. Every October, Mama and Papa visited their special areas to pick wild mushrooms. They preserved them in jars and served them fried with garlic and some tomato flavoring on holidays.

After the mushrooms, Mama served the stuffed artichokes. Nonna had prepared some cut celery stocks, finocchio (anise) portions, and a variety of nuts to be served. Aunt Lena brought two small bowls containing olive oil, salt, and black ground pepper to the table. We watched as the grown-ups dipped the finocchio or celery pieces into the oil before taking a bite off the stalk. I enjoyed only the celery with the oil. I waited for Papa to remove the walnut shells with the nutcrackers Mama provided. He passed me some walnut meat that I ate with my finocchio. Then my eyes fell on some dried figs near the bowl of fresh fruit Mama served. Like Mama, I sandwiched some walnut meat in the fig. It was a special treat.

Peter liked to tease my younger cousins and me by cutting into a pomegranate. Invariably it squirted some juice at us as he tried to separate portions of the fruit. We screamed and fussed. Papa finally gave us permission to leave the table.

The men continued their conversations while enjoying some fruit. They dunked peach pieces into their wine glasses for a few minutes before eating the peach. Uncle Sammy offered some to

---

* See "Roast Leg of Lamb p. 260

Nonna. The women preferred first to clean the many pots, pans and dishes at the sink.

"Lucia, are we gonna have coffee?" I heard Papa ask a short time later.

"Pretty soon," Mama answered.

The scent of brewing coffee filtered through the apartment. Vita, her brother Nickie and I returned to the table from the living room. We didn't want to miss tasting a piece of ricotta pie or cannoli filled with ricotta.* Maybe Mama will share a Sfogliatella or Paregini with me I thought. Everyone enjoyed the pastry.

Vita and I returned to listen to the recordings Peter was playing on the Victrola. A few hours passed before Mama called me back to the kitchen.

"Time to curl your hair," she said.

She heated the curling iron slowly on the gas burner before curling my hair and cousin Vita's, too. Then we dressed in our Easter clothes and prepared to leave for the festivities at La Sala.

Hand in hand, my cousins and I skipped down Charter Street ahead of our parents. My heart beat faster as we neared the hall doorway. We heard the music while climbing up the narrow stairway. We rushed into the noisy hall filled with music and chatter. We searched for our friends.

That evening, we concluded our Easter celebration with laughter, music, and dancing.

---

* See "Ricotta Cheese Pie" p. 320.
* See "Cannoli" p. 312.

Women and children taking part in a parade during a Saint's
Feast Day. (Circa 1930)

Poles were erected for the feast with red, green and white
banners. Scrolled wires with various colored lights extended
across the street from pole to pole along the procession route.
Photo courtesy of The Boston Restaurant Associates

Madonna Della Cava parade stopping on Charter Street.
Society members lowered the saint so the volunteers could pin
dollars to the streamers attached to the banner pole.
(Photo courtesy of Mary (DiPrimo) LoGrasso)

Neighbors enjoying a view of the feast from their apartment
windows on Charter Street.
(Photo courtesy of Mary (DiPrimo) LoGrasso)

A DAY AT THE FEAST

One bright August Sunday, when I heard the faint sound of music from the Madonna Della Cava procession, I asked Mama, "Can I go downstairs to watch the parade?"

"Si. Un vari lontano," (Yes. Don't go far) she said. "We're going to La Festa this afternoon."

I joined my friends sitting in front of the building. We waited anxiously. Though the parade was to start at noon, it took a while before it reached us on Charter Street. Each time someone donated money along the parade route, the carrier of the Madonna banner stopped. He lowered the banner for the volunteers to pin the dollars to the streamers attached to the banner pole. Then the band played "La Marcia Reale," the Italian National Anthem, before proceeding.

"Where's your sister Mary?" I asked Nettie, sitting in our doorway.

"Mary and our cousin are carrying the 'palios' today." Nettie said. "They're the Sacred Heart Banners carried alongside La Madonna," she explained.

"The palios are from Italy," Sonny said proudly.

I knew that the Madonna Della Cava Society sponsored the three-day celebration each year during the second weekend of August. But that day, I learned a history of that Madonna that I had never heard before.

"Every year, we have to listen to my father tell us the same story about the Madonna," Sonny said. "He tells us about the teenage boy in his hometown of Pietraperzia who could not talk. He had a dream that the Madonna told him to search for her portrait in the abandoned cave, and then he would be able to

123

speak. He tried to explain his dream to his mother in sign language, but she didn't understand. After the third try, he decided to look for the portrait himself. One day, he found it and ran out of the cave with the banner, crying, 'La Madonna, La Madonna – nella Cava,' pointing toward the cave."

"It was a miracle! The boy was talking!" Nettie said, interrupting her brother. "So the people kept the portrait of the Madonna holding Baby Jesus and celebrated that miracle every year with a feast. Now the people from that town celebrate it here in America."

A chill ran through me. Imagine, a boy regaining his speech.

"They're coming. I can see them down the street," MaryAnn said as she crossed over hurriedly to join us.

"They're telling us about the Madonna," I said seriously.

MaryAnn sat and listened to Sonny. "The people of the town tried to replace the banner by having a statue built. But each time a statute was made, it crumbled to pieces. The paesani (residents of the town) decided the Madonna was telling them she didn't want a statue, so it has always been a banner."

We also learned that the town's people built a Madonna Della Cava Church from donations received. The original banner remains in that church.

"Our banner is just like the original," Sonny said. "The Society members here take turns keeping it in their home."

As I looked at the colored lights above us, I realized we were celebrating something special that happened long ago and far away. Suddenly there was more meaning to the festivities and to why Mr. Mattarazzo and his men diligently worked earlier that week. They erected poles decorated with red, green, and white banners. They attached scrolled wires with various colored lights extending across the street from pole to pole along the procession route.

I became more anxious to see the Madonna again. My heart beat faster as the sound of music became louder. More people gathered on the sidewalk in front of us, so we sat on the curbstone, hoping not to soil our clothes.

"My father says it's an honor to be a part of the procession," Nettie said. "Sonny marched in it last year. This year cousin Phil and Johnny are the angels."

Soon we saw their young cousins. We called out to them, but their father instructed them to look straight ahead.

We smiled at their appearance, wearing white curly wigs, topped with a golden-edged, black, velvet, pillbox-type hat. Each wore a black velvet vest over their knee-high, light blue satin robe. Gold ribbon ties crisscrossed their legs from their golden sneakers up to their knees. They resembled pictures I had seen of young Romans in parade dress.

"My sister helped paint the gold sneakers last night," Nettie said.

We giggled and chuckled at the sight of the glittering gold rings, watches, bracelets, medals and earrings attached to their vests. We knew people devoted to the Madonna donated their jewelry to be worn by the "angels" only for the procession.

Sonny's uncle John and other committee people insisted that family members participate in the parade.

"We take turns with other boys and girls," Sonny said.

We stood up as the Madonna reached our area. I stared at the colorful, gilded portrait of the Madonna and Child with its small canopy topped with multicolored ribbon roses.

Volunteers caught the dollars thrown from apartment windows while others retrieved the change lowered in baskets. We watched the men secure the dollars onto the streamers. We stood quietly as the deafening sound of "La Marcia Reale" filled the air.

"What do they do with all that money?" Jennie asked.

"They pay their expenses and give some to charities," Sonny replied. "And they save some to build a chapel for the Madonna someday."

When the procession moved forward, we waved to Mary and her cousin carrying the palios. They smiled as they passed by.

Society members followed behind the Madonna. A large group of women in Sunday dress and barefoot walked behind them, carrying lighted candles. They recited the rosary along the procession route. Some young children dressed in white communion outfits walked with the ladies.

The sound of music slowly faded as the crowd turned onto Salem Street, heading toward Prince Street. Moving slowly behind the parade, we could see the balloon man pushing his cart filled with tinkling trinkets and whistles. He stopped for children to choose a balloon, a flag or banner. I really yearned for a blue balloon tied to my wrist to watch it float in the air. Maybe I'll get one later, I thought as he passed us.

"You know, we should have our own parade," Sonny said when the crowd dispersed.

"Let's do it tomorrow," Jennie said. "I'm going to the feast with my mother today."

"We're going, too," Cousin Josie said. "To see the angel!"

"Remember when the angel floated across the street?" I asked. "How did they do that, Sonny?"

"She wore a brace or harness that was hooked onto a pulley. That was part of the long wire that stretched across the street." Sonny explained. "Someone pulled the rope at one end and she looked like she was flying across the street. But they don't do that in this feast."

Hearing Sonny mention the angel made Josie and me more anxious to go to the festival area. We crossed the street to wait for her parents. Josie's parents, Mama's brother Uncle Jack and wife Aunt Martha met us in the bakery. They arrived shortly before Nonna and Aunt Lena and Aunt Lena's daughter Vita. Josie and I each held one of Vita's hands and led the group down Charter Street. The recent procession we had seen reached the festival area the same time we did. My body vibrated with the loud sound of the Roma Band. The committeemen halted the Madonna under an enclosed container hovering high above us over the street. The container was secured in that position by long wires wrapped around it that extended to apartment buildings on both sides of the street.

We stood on the Hanover Street sidewalk facing Battery Street, looking up at the container. Then the music stopped.

"Look toward the apartment windows across the street." Josie told Cousin Vita.

"Look for the angel," I said.

Josie and I held our breath.

"There she is! There's the angel," I shouted. I saw a young girl with her white dress and sparkling crown looking out of a third-floor window. I feared for her safety as she leaned forward to grasp the ropes that secured her to the window frame. They led to the container lids.

A hush swept over the crowd. She yanked at the ropes and the lids opened. White doves swiftly flew to freedom. Cheers, whistles, and applause broke out around us. Tears of excitement filled my eyes.

Everyone hailed, "Viva, Madonna, Viva!" And the band again played the familiar anthem.

The procession moved forward several yards on Hanover Street toward the temporary outdoor chapel and altar. The festival committee secured the Madonna banner on the altar. It remained outdoors for adoration from Friday to Sunday evening. People brought large bouquets of fresh flowers and lighted candles to place on the altar.

The band members seated themselves on the bandstand erected across the street from the Madonna Chapel.

"Can I have some cecere?" I asked Mama when I saw a familiar pushcart. She bought a small bag of dried salted chickpeas and reminded me to share them with others. Uncle Jack stopped to buy Nonna her favorite string of dried, salted and roasted filberts from another peddler as we mingled in the crowd. While we nibbled on ceci and filberts, we heard vendors shouting, "Ice cream," "Cold drinks here," "Pizza, five cents a piece," "Fresh slush, fresh slush." We could smell steamed crabs and turned towards the "crab man" as he hollered "Caudi, caudi." "We paused to watch a young man with a pushcart full of cherrystone clams prying open the clams with his small sharp knife. A crowd gathered around him. Our mouths watered as we watched men enjoy the clams with a squirt of lemon juice or a little hot sauce on top. We moved toward the scent of sausages and peppers frying. We saw people enjoying them in a sandwich. The combined aromas of all the foods around us spread through the crowd and hung heavy over the festivities throughout the hot afternoon.

Music bellowed through the amplifiers attached to the red-white-and-blue-decorated bandstand, illuminated with bright lights. We heard familiar operatic areas, concert pieces and selections of Italian and American melodies. During the band's intermissions, we listened to local singers performing from the bandstand. The entertainment continued into the evening, ending at 11 P.M. Though it disturbed mothers with young children trying to sleep, everyone endured the noise throughout the three-day celebration.

When our parents stopped to purchase a raffle ticket at the altar, I stared reverently at the beautiful Madonna and Child. I thought of the young boy who had found the banner and experienced the miracle long ago.

A society member gave each of us a pin consisting of a miniature portrait of the Madonna and Child that I happily attached to my dress.

We worked our way back through the noisy, crowded street lined with people and venders. We greeted many of our friends, as did our parents. We tried to stay close to our parents. We didn't want to become separated in the busy crowd.

Before returning to Charter Street, Papa and Uncle Jack bought each of us some slush. We really wanted a balloon tied to our wrists, but we enjoyed the slush after the salted ceci and filberts.

"Maybe we'll get a balloon at the next feast," Josie said. "There's another one next week."

While we enjoyed our cold lemony slush, my mind drifted back to the young boy who found the Madonna banner. It made me happy to know the story behind the celebration. I looked forward to the three or four more feasts to come and what else I might learn before the end of summer.

ANGEL ON HIGH

After breakfast on a Monday in August, I joined my friends Jennie, Nettie, Mary and Sonny sitting on the wrought-iron entrance steps of our apartment building. Jennie lived on the first floor. Sonny, his sisters Mary and Nettie resided on the second floor. I lived on the fourth floor.

We sat quietly watching Mr. Mattarazzo's workers remove festive lights, banners and poles that had decorated our street for the Madonna Della Cava Feast the past weekend. While they loaded everything onto their truck, we reminisced about the friends we saw in Sunday's procession and our visit to the festival area that day.

"Today is a good day to have our procession," Sonny said enthusiastically. We had briefly discussed this the day before. "We can make wings out of cardboard and cover them with tissue paper. We'll put a saint's picture on a stick and have our own celebration."

"Yea?" we cried in unison.

The tall, comical and kind teenager enjoyed organizing activities for us. He acted as our big brother.

"We're going to have our own procession!" Jennie cried out to Cousin Josie and MaryAnn as they crossed the street to join us.

"When?" they asked.

"I'm going now to get some cartons to make wings," Jennie said eagerly.

She grabbed Josie's hand and coaxed her to follow her into her grandparents' produce store in the basement of our building.

Nettie, MaryAnn and I volunteered to get change from our mothers.

When I entered the kitchen, Mama was about to hang out some of her wash through the bedroom window. Mama used that clothesline when she had only a few clothes to dry. She stopped to listen to my request. She smiled as she gave me a nickel.

"Stati vicino" (stay close by), she said.

I ran out the door and down the four flights of stairs. Sonny took the change we gave him and dashed off to purchase the paper.

Jennie and Josie soon returned with two cardboard boxes and a long stick.

"Who's going to be the angel?" MaryAnn asked when Sonny returned.

"First we'll make one set of wings. We'll try them on Vita 'cause she's the smallest," Sonny replied. "We'll use this rope to tie the wings on you, Vita. I'll hold on to the end of the rope while you and me climb up on the fire escape."

Apparently, Sonny had everything planned. Everyone listened approvingly.

At the age of nine, however, I had reservations about climbing onto the fire escape. I didn't know if I could slide off the fire escape and didn't want to say I was scared. I was shorter and smaller than my friends were and very shy. I felt the blood rush to my face in embarrassment and fear. Yet I felt pride in being the chosen one. I admired the young girl at each festival who appeared dressed as an angel. She paid homage to the saint at the finale of the procession by seemingly flying across the street. In reality though she was hooked up to a wire for safety reasons. My courage increased as I thought about the stories Mama and Nonna told me. Both had told me that each of us has a special guardian angel watching over us everyday.

We watched as Sonny cut two wing shapes from the cardboard boxes with a knife and scissors that Mary borrowed from their kitchen. Then Mary helped us cover "the wings" with white tissue paper and glue. I had borrowed glue from Papa's desk in the bakery across the street. We laughed and chatted as we worked diligently.

Sonny ran up to his apartment. He returned with a hammer, nails, and an eight-by-ten colored photograph of the Madonna.

"Are we going to add streamers to the Madonna picture?" MaryAnn asked.

"I'm cutting a few from this tissue paper," Nettie said.

Our excitement grew as Sonny secured the photograph and tissue strips to the top of the stick.

"Now we need some music," he said.

Two younger onlookers cried out, "We can find some boxes and sticks for you, Sonny – for the drums. Can we be the drummers?" asked the boys.

We realized then that Jennie's four-year-old sister, Mary, her six-year-old brother Frankie and Sonny's young brother Joey had been quietly watching us.

"Okay. You can be drummers!" Sonny said.

"And 'Little Mary,' you can hold a streamer."

Little Mary's face lit up with a bright smile.

"Let's sing, ta-da-dum, ta-da-dum, ta-da-dum with the drummers," Sonny's sister Mary added.

Soon we saw the two boys beating their empty cardboard box with a stick as they walked toward us.

Everyone practiced while Sonny worked the rope into the wings. I held onto my dress while he secured the wings on my back. He wrapped the rope over my shoulders, under my arms and across my chest. Then he tied it around my waist and held on to the remaining rope.

The fear returned. My stomach felt queasy.

"Joey and Frankie, you walk in front of Jennie. She'll carry the Saint. Josie and Little Mary, you walk beside Jennie and hold on to one of the streamers. MaryAnn and Nettie, you walk with Mary." He pointed to his sister.

As Sonny spoke, we lined up on the sidewalk. "Now walk slow, everyone," he added. "We'll walk to Unity Street and back (about 300 feet)."

"Make sure that they all sing and stay together." Sonny said to his sister Mary.

We marched proudly to "ta-da-dum, ta-da-dum." We stepped down to the street from the narrow brick sidewalk to avoid any people sitting in front of stores. Smiling faces looked down at us from apartment windows. We joyously continued singing and following Jennie.

On our return, Sonny directed us into the courtyard beside our tenement. We marched around to the rear and then to the opposite side of the building. Each of us shrugged our noses at the disturbing odor still lingering from the garbage barrels. That morning, the landlord had moved them to the sidewalk for the Monday pick up. Our procession continued to the foot of the fire escape.

My heart pounded with anxiety as I heard Sonny say, "I'll lift you up, Vita. You'll be safe. I have the rope in my hand."

The singing and drumming continued as Sonny helped me onto the fire escape landing.

"I'm ready, Vita." he said.

Sonny signaled for silence.

With my heart still pounding, I sat on the landing. I slowly eased myself to the edge, dangling my legs and sliding closer toward the edge, ready to leave the landing. I felt a pain from the rope tightening around my chest and waist as Sonny secured the rope ends tightly in his hands.

Jennie lifted the Madonna's photo into the air. Everyone waited to hear me hail, "Viva, Madonna, Viva!" Instead we heard, "Veeeeee Taaaaa." That terrifying scream from the fourth-floor window interrupted our performance. Pain wrenched my chest as I briefly dangled, panic stricken in the air. "Jump!" Sonny shouted as he let go of the rope. Instantly I fell into Mary's outstretched arms. Sonny jumped to the ground. He removed the rope and wings. Everyone departed swiftly. In my head, I heard, it's Mama, it's Mama. I bolted into the building through the rear door and up the stairs as fast as possible, though fearful of the outcome. As I breathlessly reached the last step, I saw

Mama with a red face and glaring eyes waiting for me at the kitchen door. She pointed silently to the kitchen chair. I sheepishly slid into the chair and sat in dead silence, asking myself, why did Mama scream?

I have no recollection of Mama ever discussing that event with me. But I do remember spending the entire day with her, quietly waiting hours for her to speak. In later years, when I understood the danger of that activity, I realized that her thoughts of what could have happened frightened her into silence. I'm grateful that my angel, Mama, came to the window that day.

Infant Jesus — A gift from Sicily sent to Vita by her maternal grandmother.

A CHRISTMAS STORY

I don't recall any exchange of Christmas gifts at our family gatherings in Boston's North End, known as "Little Italy." When I was young, and family friends hadn't yet adopted that American tradition. On Christmas Eve we gathered with family members to bake, cook, and share the foods prepared for the Christmas Holiday. However, that doesn't mean that my brother Peter and I didn't dream of Santa Claus arriving with gifts for us someday.

During the Great Depression days of the 1930s, I recall my friends saying, "I went with my father today to get our bread and milk."

That seemed strange. I recalled having seen their parents occasionally buying milk in our store. Papa explained that many families in our community suffered from unemployment at that time. They swallowed their Italian pride and waited in the long "bread lines" at a designated area for free bread and milk. These conditions saddened everyone.

I remember Papa hiring young teenage boys to work on the delivery trucks or in the bakery. They earned money and a loaf of bread for the family.

In December, we waited for pleasant occurrences. One incident before Christmas was the arrival of the large truck that parked in front of our family bakery. My brother Peter and I joined the crowd outside. We watched as one of the men in the truck called out the names of the food basket recipients. I've never forgotten the smiling faces and teary eyes of the adults walking home with their holiday food.

"How did they know where to find these people?" I asked

Peter. I was only six or seven years old. Yet I wondered, where did these truckers get these names?

"The newspapers receive names of families who need help during the holiday," Peter answered. "People send them the money for the gifts they give away."

An evening or two later, another truck arrived. Again we waited for the men to lift the tarpaulin that blocked our view of the contents. While one held a wrapped toy, another man called out a child's name. Screams of joy filled the air. Each youngster responded with screams of joy as he or she pushed through the crowd to receive the gift. I felt my heart beat fast, hoping I might be a recipient.

Once when the truck left and my brother and I had not received anything again, I asked Peter, "How come we never get anything?"

Disgruntled, Peter turned to me and said, "Because Pa won't send in our names." He paused a second and then said, "But we get new clothes don't we? Some of these kids don't."

Unbeknown to us, Mama heard our conversation. "And you do have bread on your table. Some families aren't that lucky," she added.

We quietly followed her into the bakery.

"Vita, I have something to show you." Mama said to me a few minutes later. Confused but excited, I went with Mama to our apartment. In her bedroom, I watched as she searched in her large trunk. She pulled out a small rolled-up blanket.

"This is yours," she said. She smiled and put the bundle in my hands.

"Your Nonna Vita in Sicily sent this to you after you were born."

My eyes opened wide. My hands shook while I walked toward the kitchen table to unwrap the blanket. I stared in disbelief at the beautiful blue-eyed Baby Jesus figure dressed only in a tiny diaper. His arms stretched out, waiting for me to hold him. I couldn't speak.

"In our village, people gather on Christmas Eve for a procession before the evening Mass," Mama said. "They carry lighted candles and sing hymns all the way to church. After Mass they have an annual church raffle. Nonna Vita won this Infant Jesus the December that you were born.

Every Christmas season I display that beautiful gift in my home, and I say a prayer of thanks to my Nonna Vita for being my Santa Claus that year.

Vita's granddaughter Kristina Meuse helping to cut Strufoli as
Vita fries them. Photo by Sinopoli Family,1999

A display of Vita's traditional Christmas cookies. Pictured are
Vita's Cannalicchi Fig Cookies, Christmas Fruitcake and
"Regina" Sesame Seed Cookies.
Photo by Sinopoli family,1999.

A FAMILY TRADITION
ON CHRISTMAS EVE

It was not the custom in our family during the 1930s and '40s to exchange Christmas gifts. The tradition was to bake and cook enough for the holiday table and to share food with relatives and friends.

Some of my most gratifying memories of Christmas are of hours spent in the home of Papa's uncle whom we called Zio Nino (Uncle Antonino).

The family lived in a fourth-floor apartment above Papa's bakery on Charter Street in the North End of Boston. I enjoyed watching his wife, Zia Marianna, her four daughters and Mama preparing and baking Christmas desserts.

Zio Nino was a surrogate father to Papa and his brother, Joe. Their widowed mother was his sister. She resided in Sicily near two married daughters.

During Christmas week Papa's uncle purchased four pounds of dried figs and ground them in his meat grinder. He added wine and black ground pepper to the mixture used in making Cannalicchi.

My maternal grandmother and Zia Marianna had been childhood friends in Sicily where they learned the art of making these fig tarts. Each year Zia invited Nonna to come with Mama two evenings before Christmas to help make the traditional Cannalicchi.* Four women sat one at each side of a large square wooden board, which they rested on their thighs just as they had done in their homeland.

Zia's oldest daughter, Marion, and Mama cut and rolled walnut-size pieces of dough. They placed a tablespoon of the mixture in the

---

See "Cannalicchi" p.308

center. I marveled at how Nonna and Zia delicately crimped and pleated the dough around the fig mixture, creating a tart. They reminisced as they worked, and I learned about their lives in Italy.

Zia's daughters Vita and Anna placed the tarts on trays that their father placed in their black Glenwood stove oven, two trays at one time, to bake. The sweet aroma of wine and figs filled the room. Soon we heard my great aunt say, "Nino sono cotti?" (Nino, are they cooked)?

My mouth watered but I knew not to ask for one yet. I waited until Cousins Vita and Anna prepared and served coffee later with some Cannalicchi. Nonna was given a bowlful to take home.

Christmas Eve morning, Mama blended water, yeast, oil, salt and flour by hand in a large pan. Zio Nino delivered the Sfingi* (sfeengee) mixture to his wife, who punched the dough down three or four times that day.

That afternoon Mama and I went to Zio's apartment. Zia was kneading the dough for the ricotta-filled turnovers called Cassattedi.* They look like large ravioli. Mama mixed some orange rinds into the ricotta. As she stirred the mixture, Uncle Joe's wife, Zia Nina, arrived with her two young daughters, Vita and Santa, and another paesana (friend from the hometown). She handed Zia Marianna a large platter of fried baccala that she brought for hors d'oeurves. Then four of the ladies sat at the large lapboard. They painstakingly rolled, filled and sealed the turnovers. Then with a light touch with the fork tip they secured the ricotta in the Cassattedi. Zia Marianna prepared to fry the Cassattedi. When Zia browned them on each side in her skillet, the seam sometimes opened and ricotta spilled into the oil. We heard hissing and splattering. Our eyes became teary and burned.

"Open the door and windows," Zia cried out. She cleaned out the skillet and added oil and continued frying.

Her daughter Josie and my brother Peter were the same age— four years older. With patience she allowed me to sprinkle granulated

* See "Sfingi" p. 314

sugar on the fried Cassattedi with her. I yearned to eat one from the platter but waited.

All afternoon family friends arrived for brief visits to extend holiday greetings. Zia Marianna made sure the visitors departed with some of her holiday pastries. They brought homemade goodies from their home. The women continued to work at the large square table while Anna and Josie served coffee, baccala, Cannalicchi and Cassattedi to the friends. Some of those in the neighborhood whom Zia didn't see were sent a small serving of the same. I sometimes followed Josie while she made deliveries. I felt like a Christmas elf greeting "Buono Natale" as we handed them the goodies.

The tenements permeated with a mixture of aromas. We recognized the strong scent of stuffed quahogs, razor clams and shrimp generously garnished with garlic, olive oil, bread crumbs and parsley. The scent seeped through open doors and windows. It blended with the distinctive odor of pesce stocco,* (stock fish) in tomato sauce flavored with capers, bay leaf, celery and potatoes to be served as suppers. Fish was our main meal on Christmas Eve because of the holiday fast.

Mama had reminded us to stop in the bakery to bring up the calamari* she had stuffed and baked earlier. When we entered Zia's kitchen I heard Mama say, "E pronti." (It is ready). She was checking the Sfingi dough.

"Lucy, the oil is also ready," Marion said.

Mama dipped one hand into the soft mixture, squeezed a small portion through a clenched fist, and spooned it into the oil. Each spoonful rose as a golden brown ball that Marion scooped out and placed into a bowl filled with sugar. Josie and I spread more sugar over them while someone opened the kitchen door to let the odor of frying dough escape.

"Now this smells like Christmas." I soon heard Papa say as he entered the kitchen.

Papa, Peter, and Uncle Joe followed Zio Nino and his two sons,

---

* See "Pesce Stocco" p. 208
* See "Calamari (Squid) in Tomato Sauce over Linguine" p. 202

Peter and Tony. They brought up several loaves of fresh bread from the bakery. Shortly after, Zia Marianna's brother Paul and family of four arrived to join us for supper. They brought a platter of Strufoli.* Everyone ate some of the golden nuggets covered with honey and nonpareils.

The extended kitchen table was not large enough to seat everyone for supper. It didn't matter. We enjoyed being together. The young children sat on a parent's lap while others stood near a counter to eat

Though I ate some fish and bread, I yearned for the desserts made once a year. While the ladies cleared the kitchen of dishes, pots, and pans a sampling of Cassattedi, Cannalicchi, Sfingi, Strufoli, and Baccala remained on the kitchen table together with coffee, soft drinks, wine and a variety of nuts and fruit.

The youngsters waited for Zio Nino to bring out the Lotto box. Some joined us and stayed to play a game or two of Lotto. The Italian Bingo game entertained us all night. Family friends continued to arrive with holiday greetings. Some joined us and stayed to play a game or two of Lotto.

I sat on Papa's lap and tried to remain awake until we departed for home or to attend midnight Mass. When Nonna was with us, I sometimes left with her to attend the midnight Mass. All four Catholic Churches in the community served a midnight Mass.

Nonna and I walked three blocks to Saint Anthony's Church on Prince Street. We sat close to the altar with her lady friends. Before the Mass they recited the rosary in Italian. Parishioners joined then in singing the Christmas carols during the services.

When they sang Tu Scendi Delle Stelle, tears filled my eyes. I stared at the beautiful manger as they sang slowly, like praying. An aura of reverence filled the church and me, long to be remembered.

---

* See "Strufoli" p. 324

THE MOVIES

When I saw the men entering the bakery carrying large movie posters, I waited to hear Mama ask, "Any passes today?" We used the passes to see the movies playing in the vicinity.

Mama placed the three or four posters in our large bakery window.

I learned to love the movies early in life. While my brother attended with his friends, I enjoyed movies with my parents, as a young girl. Later, I walked with my teenage cousins and friends to the movie theaters every weekend.

It took us approximately twenty minutes to reach either the Scollay, Bowdoin, Rialto, Casino, or Lancaster theaters. For ten cents, we lost ourselves in the story shown on the silver screen. Continuous showings gave us the option to see the movie a second time before leaving.

To reach the "uptown" theaters on Washington and Tremont Street, we planned a thirty-minute walk. We asked each other, "Do you have your hat pin?" Our mothers told us to secure it inside our jacket or hat. I always had one in my purse ready for use if anyone bothered us at any time.

"Some kids are visiting the Rialto today," we heard on school days.

The rumor spread quickly when students played "hooky." Girls like myself attending Girls' High School and boys going to English High School both traveled on the same streetcars. Both schools were located off Tremont Street in the South End.

Those playing "hooky" relished the day watching the old cowboy thrillers at the Rialto. Sometimes they sneaked into the

Old Howard or Crawford House during afternoon burlesque shows.

The Rialto remained open daily for twenty-four hours. It was one I never attended because of stories I heard from my brother Peter.

"A lot of the homeless people sleep in there—and alcoholics, too." he said.

I remember him saying, "We did plenty of howling and whistling today," when he returned with friends.

"That was some fight scene in the saloon with Tom Mix. We really got carried away, didn't we?" the boys boasted.

"We woke up all the winos and poor people sleeping." Peter bragged.

I listened to their exhilarating descriptions of the Indian chases, train robberies, and the arrival of the rescuing "good guys" with the white hats.

"Nobody paid attention to the ushers today," Peter snickered.

At the Bowdoin, Lancaster, and Casino theaters, ushers walked up and down the aisles when the crowds became rowdy. They whacked a big stick along the rows of wooden seats. Everyone in those seats felt their body vibrate.

During amateur shows at the Casino or Lancaster theaters, the loud boos and howls for a performer resulted in having the audition master walk onto the stage. He pulled the amateur performer off the stage with his long-handled hook. The audience then whistled and clapped with approval.

The highlight of our school week came on Friday night. We gathered on Michelangelo Terrace around 6 P.M. at the site of our Junior High School known to us as "The Mickies." When the auditorium doors opened at 7 P.M., bedlam ensued. Youngsters pushed and shoved to get inside the building to pay our nickel fee. We scrambled for the front row seats. Teenagers rushed upstairs to the balcony for more private seating. The manager and adults bellowed, "Slow down—don't push!" Those words fell on deaf ears.

A few destructive boys in the balcony removed slats from chairs and used them as drumsticks during the evening. Some of those rowdies occasionally tossed down a "stink bomb." The elders became embarrassed and angry. Everyone sneered at the foul odor.

"I want to remind you that I will stop the movie if this or any other incidence occurs. Don't spoil it for everyone," the manager pleaded.

The loud whistling continued as boys and girls stomped their feet for the presentation to begin. The manager again called for silence. Finally the lights lowered. The gentle fingers of the pianist danced over the piano keyboard simultaneously with the actions in the silent movie.

The story flickering on the silver screen enthralled us. Laughter filled the hall with the amusing actions of Charlie Chaplin, Buster Keaton, Ben Turpin, Laurel and Hardy or the Keystone Cops. Then we traveled out west with Tom Mix, Tom Tyler, Buster Crabbe, Leo Carrillo, Wm. S. Hart, or Bob Steele. A brief intermission led to one or two cartoons. The blunders, buffoonery and travesties of Mickey Mouse, Felix the Cat, or Popeye fascinated us. An occasional old "talking" movie featuring George Raft, Jean Harlow, The Little Rascals, Mary Pickford or John Barrymore pleased us.

The last feature to be seen on Fridays was the "chapter picture." Piano music accompanied the actions in the silent series. We sat spellbound, especially with scenes like the lifeless body of our heroine stretched across the railroad track. We held our breath as we saw a train come closer and closer to the fallen heroine. The pianist played faster and faster — then stopped abruptly. The screen flashed "TO BE CONTINUED." That ended our Friday entertainment.

As Easter neared each year, we waited to see Cecil B. deMille's silent classic, *KING OF KINGS*.

Around 1937, the Scollay, Bowdoin, Lancaster and Casino theaters offered pieces of china edged in 18-karat gold. My friends and I happily accompanied our mothers on Wednesday or Thursday afternoons, though we preferred to attend without them. For fifty cents, we enjoyed the Pathe News, a movie, coming attractions and a cartoon. We returned home with welcomed china used on special occasions.

New movie releases opened at the Metropolitan on Tremont Street (now Wang Center); or the R.K.O. Keith's Memorial (later the Boston Opera House); or Paramount Theater on Washington Street. After a week's showing, it transferred to another theater in the area. As youngsters, we waited until the movie played at the Scollay, Modern, Beacon, Bowdoin or Lancaster where we paid only a ten-cent fee. In later years, we treated ourselves to the elegantly decorated Loews Orpheum, Paramount, R.K.O. Keith's Memorial or Metropolitan theaters. They resembled palaces or grand opera houses. We purchased our fifty cents ticket and handed it to the uniformed door attendant. Our eyes quickly focused on the plush carpeted runners over marbled floors and stairs. I felt guilty putting my hands on the bright shiny brass staircase railings. I remember the glittering chandeliers, gilded moldings, and colorful wall and ceiling murals. Another uniformed usher, with a tiny flashlight, guided us to our plush velvety balcony seats. The magnificent interiors of these buildings and the stories we saw unfolding on the screen transported us to a dreamland. We forgot temporarily about the cold-water flats we called home in Boston's North End.

MUSICAL MEMORIES

Everyday, I listened to the radio as I sat on my perch, watching Papa, Mama and the bakers at work. The radio rested on a shelf beside me. Each week, we waited to listen to the popular Hit Parade Program. Peter and I were familiar with many songs because our parents played their recordings by Italian and American artists often on our hand-cranked Victrola in our apartment. They had started their record collection in the 1920s. Music became part of our life.

I never dreamed I would see or meet many of the musical artists in person. It all started one Sunday about 1936. "I have tickets to see Paul Whitman at the Boston Garden tonight," Papa told us. Our family had often enjoyed his radio broadcasts. We sat in the balcony to one side of the large orchestra seated on stage below us. Paul Whitman, a tall, robust man carrying a long baton, appeared on stage. As he directed with his baton, the orchestra played. We were enthralled with beautiful music like George Gershwin's "Rhapsody in Blue" and Grofe's "Grand Canyon Suite." I have loved these compositions since that night.

A short time later, we saw at the Metropolitan Theater live performances by Jimmy Durante and his cast. Included was an unforgettable rendition of "Mr. Paganini" sung by a new singer-comedian named Martha Raye. She became a star in a few brief years. She visited the North End restaurants often, as did many other performers including Jimmy Durante, Enrico Caruso and Ezio Pinza during Boston engagements.

My friends and I thought of Washington, Boylston, and Tremont streets as our Broadway. North Enders referred to that area as "uptown" and considered it part of our home territory because of its close proximity to our tiny community. We attended early afternoon performances on Saturday or Sunday. Our purpose was to spend time at the backstage door of the R.K.O. Boston. The theater, located on Heywood Place off Washington Street, also became a stopover for us on our way home from Girls' High School. The school was on West Newton Street off Tremont Street in Boston's South End. We walked about a mile and a half down Tremont Street to the Metropolitan Theater (now Wang Center). We read all the billboards, showing what movies currently played and those soon to come. Then we proceeded next door to the Wilbur Theater and across the street to the Shubert Theater.

Theaters in Boston gave local residents a chance to view new stage plays and musicals before reaching Broadway. My friend Phyllis and I saw Rogers and Hammerstein's *Allegro* at the Shubert Theater. Some of the music was heartrending. The show pleased us, but we soon learned that it would endure changes and rewrites. In 1943 it emerged as *Carousel.* It became a very successful stage show that still featured the songs "You'll Never Walk Alone" and "My Boy Bill."

The afternoons we stopped at the backstage door of the R.K.O. Boston, we waited to get a glimpse of performers and obtain autographs when they exited on coffee breaks or dinner breaks. It was there that we spoke with the slender, smiling, blue-eyed Helen O'Connell and handsome Bob Eberly. We expressed how much we enjoyed their recordings of "Green Eyes" and "Marie Elena" with Jimmy Dorsey's Band. We told Vaughn Monroe that his version of "There I've Said It Again" and his theme song, "Racing with the Moon" was two of our favorite recordings. Another day we met the Dead End Kids returning from a coffee break. We told them we lived in the North End.

"We were there for supper last night," they said as they mingled with us on that narrow street.

"Is Frank Sinatra coming out?" we asked the Pied Pipers when they exited one afternoon.

"He has his meals indoors," they told us. We waited in line

over an hour to purchase orchestra tickets. We planned to sit close to the stage to see Frank Sinatra. We screamed and swooned with all the other bobbysocksers as he sang "I'll Never Smile Again," "Imagination," and "I'll Be Seeing You." His slender body leaned on the microphone and our hearts fluttered as he swayed from side to side. We remembered when he first sang with Harry James before joining Tommy Dorsey's orchestra. That week we returned to see him again. We hurried to the backstage door at the end of the live performance but left with disappointment at not seeing him exit the stage door. Later we learned that he used another exit to return to the hotel.

We paid fifty cents during the day and seventy-five cents in the evening to see bands like Artie Shaw, Benny Goodman, Count Basie, the DorseyBand, Duke Ellington, Eddie Duchin, Harry James, Glenn Miller, Lionel Hampton and their singers. The theater presented a cartoon, and Pathe or Movietone news clips, and a feature movie before the live performances. A comic act appeared first on stage like Martha Raye, Abbot and Costello or Henny Youngman with his violin. Live acrobatic acts, animal acts, magicians like Harry Blackstone, or tap dancers like the Nicholas Brothers or Buddy Ebsen entertained us on stage before the band and singers performed. Sometimes the theater presented a special attraction along with a live band performance. It was delightful to see and listen to vocalists like Vic Damone, Eddie Fisher, The Andrews Sisters, Rosemary Clooney, Doris Day, The Mills Brothers, Ink Spots, Billie Holiday and Ella Fitzgerald.

Those happy days waiting at the backstage door soon became somber days after the Pearl Harbor attack. Many neighborhood boys talked about volunteering after graduation in June 1942. Some even left high school and college early that year to enter the services, as did my brother Peter and his friends.

While at camp in North Carolina, Peter became a friend with a fellow sergeant whose name I have forgotten. He lived off base with his wife. They invited Peter to dinner often. Kitty Kallen, the wife's sister, visited them one day when appearing at a local army base. Her sister was her acting manager in her early career.

Peter learned that Kitty Kallen's sister was trying to arrange a contract for her to appear at the R.K.O. Boston. When Kitty's sister came to Boston to finalize the engagement, she called our apartment. Mama invited her to dinner. I'm sure Peter had told her how many times I attended live performances at that theater. After supper, our guest thanked Mama for supper and invited me to visit Kitty Kallen backstage during her stay in Boston.

"And bring your girl friend, too," she said, pointing to Josie, who had joined us for supper that evening.

It was an exhilarating experience walking through the backstage door of the R.K.O. Boston a few weeks later. It seemed like a dream, entering Kitty Kallen's dressing room. She greeted us warmly and apologized for working on her gown as we talked in the tiny room. Josie and I just stared in amazement at the beautifully decorated gowns on a rack along one wall.

"I do all my own decorating because it is very expensive to have someone sew sequins and beads on gowns," she explained. "Besides, it keeps me busy between performances. It becomes very lonesome traveling," she said. "I like it better when my sister is with me."

She thanked us for coming. We left her room with an autographed photo and a feeling of knowing she had really enjoyed our visit. We couldn't wait to see her perform.

In 1940, a local radio station offered a free autographed recording by Harry James to the listener who first called in the correct name of the song played. Papa laughed as I made the call from the bakery, never believing I would be the first caller. I was and proudly walked the next day to Krey's Music Store on Washington Street with my girl friends. We watched the tall, fashionably dressed Harry James smile and autograph my copy of *The Carnival of Venice*.

During the war years, The R.K.O. Keith's Memorial Theater (across from the R.K.O. Boston) treated audiences between movies with special organ music by John Kiley. We knew him as our organist at St. Stephen's Church on Hanover Street. He also played the Star Spangled Bianner before Celtics and Boston Bruins games at the Boston Garden. We thoroughly enjoyed seeing John Kiley and the organ slowly rise from the orchestra pit between movies at that theater. Loud musical notes filled the air. We watched the screen and sang loudly, following the bouncing ball on the words of "Let me Call You Sweetheart," "Daisy, Daisy," "My Wild Irish Rose," "The Band Played On," "When Irish Eyes Are Smiling," "Yankee Doodle Dandy" and "Over There." Those musical moments brightened our moods after having viewed the disturbing news clips of encounters our servicemen and women endured each day.

A memorable stage-door experience occurred in the fall of 1942. After school we waited at the stage door to see members of the Glenn Miller orchestra. On our third attempt, before entering the theater, we spoke with the Modernaires on their return from a coffee break. We congratulated the tall, handsome Tex Benecke and the blue-eyed, smiling Marion Hutton on their great performance of "Chattanooga Choo Choo."

While we waited for autographs, a truck pulled up near us. The driver entered the backstage door and came out within a few minutes. He recognized some members of Glenn Miller's band and shouted, "Hey, I have the snowballs!"

"Snowballs?" we asked.

"Yes," they explained. "They're for the promotion of our new movie, *Sun Valley Serenade* with Sonja Henie."

At that time I noticed my friend Phyllis speaking to Chuck Goldstein of the Modernaires. Chuck seemed unconcerned about the snowballs. Instead he walked towards me and said, "Sing for me. She told me you wrote a song for us. I'd like to hear it."

I was astonished. "Me, sing here on the street?" I said. No way, I thought. Mama and Papa would not be happy. But Phyllis and our other four friends encouraged me, especially since Chuck said he had time. They formed a circle around Chuck and me. My body trembled and the voice cracked but I managed to sing "What Happens on a Moonlight Night." When I got to the last two lines, Chuck joined me in the final repetitive lines of my arrangement. Everyone clapped and cheered.

Though breathless, shaking and startled, I heard him say enthusiastically, "If we weren't breaking up after next week's show in New York, I'd ask you for a copy."

I couldn't believe he sang with me, but more disbelieving were his words "breaking up."

"Captain Miller has already enlisted," he added. "He'll be traveling with an Air Force Band to entertain the troops." We learned that other band members, excluding Chuck, had also enlisted.

We returned to see their last three evening performances. Tears rolled down our faces each time. We left with deep sorrow the last night as the curtain slowly closed while they played "The Moonlight Serenade." Those evenings at the R.K.O Boston flash in my mind each time I play his recordings or hear Glenn Miller's music on the radio. A few years later we mourned with thousands at the news of Captain Miller's fatal airplane crash.

During the war years, we attended several bond rallies held at the Boston Garden. One that remains vivid in my mind was an appearance by Bob Hope and his tour group. That evening Jerry Colona, Marylyn Maxwell, Martha Raye, and Jimmy Durante entertained us along with acrobatic and dancing performers. One unforgettable moment was when the clapping, cheering and teary-eyed audience stood up to thank Kate Smith for her electrifying performance of Irving Berlin's "God Bless America."

After the war, we attended dances at the Roseland State Ballroom, the Frolics, Blinstrub, the Totem Pole, The Bradford Hotel, the Starlight Ballroom, the Tic Toc, to mention a few. It was thrilling to dance to the music we loved, played by the musicians who recorded it. Those pleasurable experiences remain in my heart forever.

The sight of the 700 foot Trylon needle set near the huge 200 foot Perisphere was astonishing.

We saw the most spectacular highly polished, slim silver and black "Train of Tomorrow" with oval rather than square cars.

We stood in awe of the 250 foot Lifesaver Parachute Jump.

Our last stop was at the top of the Empire State Building, then the tallest building in the world.

OUR WORLD'S FAIR TRIP

My parents talked so much about their visit to the Fair in 1939 that I couldn't wait for Labor Day in 1940. Mama told me she had asked Aunt Lena if cousin Vita could join us for the trip. I was fifteen and Vita was five years younger. Because she lived close by, she was like a sister and often my companion in our home.

Papa drove us from Boston to New York in our Oldsmobile early Saturday morning. My brother Peter was left in charge at the bakery, with our uncles checking in during the day. Our first stop was a bed and breakfast in Flushing, New York, where my parents had previously stayed. It had been a long five-hour trip since five-thirty that morning. Cousin Vita and I looked forward to a hamburger at the Fair, which Papa had promised us earlier.

After registering, we departed for the Fair. We waited patiently in the long line to pay fifty cents each for our tickets. Our hearts were pounding with excitement as we went through the gates.

The sight of the 700-foot Trylon needle set near the huge 200-foot Perisphere was astonishing. I have never forgotten that moment.

Papa soon found a place for us to have our long-awaited hamburger. Then we walked to the Railroad Exhibit. We sat in an amphitheater to view the "Train of Tomorrow Show." Several old train cars from the 1800s passed by us on a track. We saw a series of different shapes and sizes. Then came a most spectacular highly polished, slim, silver and black "Train of Tomorrow" with oval, rather than square cars. It looked so different from the black coal-burning "iron horse" with box-shaped cars seen in movies and at Boston's North and South Stations.

"Where are we going next?" Vita asked.

"We're going to see something you've never seen before," Papa said excitedly.

We followed my parents into a building where a gentleman directed us to stand in line.

"When you reach the table with a square metal box on it, look into the screen (the glass front)," he said. "A camera will focus on you," he explained.

Vita and I couldn't wait to reach the table. When we did, we were shocked at seeing ourselves on the television screen. We both giggled nervously at our appearance and then moved on.

As we walked down the corridor I heard a strange voice. Then I saw a human-size silver robot named "Elektro." It startled us to hear the talking robot greeting people in a weird voice. A cigarette rested between his lips.

"Look, it's smoking!" Vita exclaimed. In disbelief we watched the robot exhale a puff of smoke from its mouth.

Later I saw Papa purchase tickets to attend the Billy Rose Aquacade Show. My heart beat faster because Mama had told me how fascinated she had been with the show. I realized why as Vita and I sat mesmerized by the sleek, smooth precision movements of Esther Williams and her "Aquafemmes." Their bodies slid in and out of the water to the sound of music. The clear blue water sparkled with the sun's rays.

Next we visited the merry-go-round-milking platform in the Borden Building.

"Look at the cows. Let's get closer," I said as I took hold of my cousin's hand and moved through the crowd to get up front.

Vita stood speechless. She had never seen cows being milked. I wanted to see Elsie, the famous Borden Cow, but was disappointed to find she was not there that day.

From there we went to the Silex and Planters Peanut Exhibit. I was familiar with the symbol of Mr. Peanut, having seen it the previous year while visiting relatives in Albany, NY. My cousin stood wide-eyed and speechless as we stopped to look at the tall, golden-colored, metal, peanut-shaped "person" on display. The smiling Mr.

Peanut wore a monocle, a black top hat, and held a black cane in his hand. Then Mama encouraged us to move toward a table where we were given sample packages of peanuts. We enjoyed some with the ice cream that we were served.

At the Firestone Exhibit, Papa purchased an ashtray. The miniature black rubber tire with a small glass insert is now a reminder in my home of that day.

That evening we returned to the Lagoon of Nations for the choreographed performance of varied-colored lights over the Lagoon. The lights flashed over fountain sprays that raised and lowered to different heights in time to the rhythm of the music. Later, during the spectacular fireworks display, Vita and I had to cup our hands over our ears. They were even louder and more frightening than the man-made thunder and lightening that we sat through at the General Electric Exhibit.

The second day we visited the widely acclaimed General Motors "Futurama" exhibit. Seated in an armchair on a conveyor belt, we viewed the "Shape of Tomorrow" – a fifteen-minute seated tour. It displayed various-shaped automobiles being considered for manufacturing. We also saw what a community in the suburb of a city might look like in the future. It was sprinkled with wooden and brick single homes, lawns and trees on streets without stores, so different from our North End neighborhood. Also exhibited were samples of highways, wider roads and bridges for faster commuting.

Next we saw the 250-foot LifeSaver Parachute Jump where we stood in awe for several minutes. I wondered if someone would fall. I even looked back with curiosity as we walked to the next exhibit. I know I would never attempt that jump, I thought.

At the crowded Italian Pavilion, I remember seeing a row of craftsmen, each in opened individual cubicles. I was particularly interested in the glassblowers.

"How do they do that?" Vita asked.

"Just watch and you'll see," Mama whispered firmly.

The concentration and artistry of the glassblowers, the heating and twirling of the glass to create tiny intricate glass figures of animals, bottles, and cups intrigued us. My cousin and I didn't want to leave.

The Statue of Liberty was our destination on the third day. A thrill swept over me during the ferry ride. I thought of the happiness that my parents must have experienced when they first saw the statue. They had arrived in New York Harbor as immigrants from Italy at different times during the early 1900s.

"Do you want to go to the top with us?" my parents asked.

"Yes," we quickly answered. Soon we were standing in the crown of the Statue, looking out over the New York harbor. The view from the windows of the crown was spectacular.

Before returning to the ferry, Mama bought my cousin and me a small bronze replica of the Statue of Liberty as a souvenir. Vita kept hers for years, but mine was lost during the times we moved from one apartment to another. During the ride back on the ferry, I took a photograph of the scenic panorama of the New York skyline, so different from Boston.

Our last stop before leaving the city was at the Empire State Building, then the tallest building in the world.

"Look," I called to Mama, pointing to the Trylon and LifeSaver Parachute in the distance. It amazed me that we could see that far so clearly from the top of the Empire State Building.

Later that afternoon, on our way home, Vita and I reminisced about all we had seen. I did wonder if some of the changes predicted by exhibitors at the Fair might take place in our lifetime. Some did, like the number of people purchasing a television for their home, the new suburban areas that sprouted outside of Boston, the variety of automobiles seen on the roads, the faster streamline trains, and the elevated and wide highways built to bypass increasing city traffic. All those have been reminders of our exciting trip to the 1940 New York World's Fair.

CHANGES IN OUR LIVES

"Pa, turn on the radio. Something's happened," Peter called out as he ran towards the car to join us.

My parents and I were waiting in our automobile eager to leave for Fitchburg, Massachusetts. It was Sunday, December 7, 1941.

On the radio, we heard the devastating news that the Japanese had bombed Pearl Harbor. "Where's Pearl Harbor?" we asked each other.

Ironically, we were on our way that afternoon to welcome Cousin Frank home, after completing his army draftee tour of duty. Later, at Aunt Marion's home in Fitchburg, we learned that all servicemen's passes and leaves, including Frank's were cancelled. What was to be a happy reunion turned out to be a day we would never forget.

Cousin Frank didn't visit his home again until just before shipping out to Italy months later.

Everyone found rationing difficult. We had to use government-issued coupons to purchase butter, sugar, flour, eggs, oil or gasoline.

"At least we can get some here," I heard Mama say to complaining customers. "There are people in the world who are a lot worse off than we are."

In 1942 my girl friends and I enjoyed wearing bobbysocks. However we did feel "grown-up" when we occasionally wore a pair of silk stockings. But I was forever checking the stocking seams that ran up the back of the leg. I was embarrassed whenever I found myself walking in stockings with crooked seams. Because the war caused a restriction on the use of silk, a happy change occurred. While visiting our favorite Jim's Hosiery Store on Salem Street, I remember the dismay on a customer's face when the sales clerk showed her "nylon stockings." To my joy that day I learned that nylon stockings came without seams. I was very happy and excited to wear those stockings that I had.

Changes seemed to take place daily in all our lives after the Pearl Harbor bombing. Eligible draftees waited anxiously for their "greetings" from the government, calling them to duty. The Draft Board became extremely busy processing papers for those called and those volunteering.

In the fall of 1941, Papa's large bakery business had failed, partially from years of over-extended credit to customers during the depression years. By March of 1942, through the encouragement and credit backing of a friend, Papa was able to open a smaller operation on Battery Street in the North End.

As a senior at Girls' High School in 1942, I remember hearing about some of my North End classmates volunteering into the WACS and WAVES. Some enrolled in nursing schools, and later entered the Nursing Corps.

At our senior prom in June, I learned that my escort Jimmy and eight out of the ten boys in our group of friends had already volunteered to serve in the Marines after graduation. That spread a cloud of sadness during our senior prom night.

Our community had many children of Italian immigrant families eligible to be drafted. A number of them had children who had never become American citizens.

Mussolini's decision not to join the Allies in WWII caused great emotional distress in the homes and hearts of Italian families. Some were torn between the love of their homeland and their children fighting for the United States.

"I don't want my son to serve in the Italian Army," I heard as customers vehemently expressed their anger to my parents. But those of qualifying age who had not become American citizens had to decide what to do. Some of our friends received their notices from Italy and sadly departed for their homeland. Many others volunteered to serve for the United States. This brought sorrow and grief to their parents who wondered if their son might end up in combat with a relative. My heart ached for those parents; but I was equally saddened to say "goodbye" to those leaving our neighborhood to serve for America.

My brother Peter volunteered at the completion of his second year at Boston University. Before leaving in July 1942, we reminisced about how many times we had heard Papa say that he had refused to go back to Italy when summoned in 1917. Though his mother and two sisters remained in Italy, Papa joined the United States Army.

"I wanted to become a citizen here in America." Papa had told us proudly. He became a naturalized citizen at Fort Devens the day after volunteering. Papa and Mama quietly accepted Peter's decision to leave college and enter the Army Air Force.

As the weeks and months passed, we learned about Papa's nephew Vito, his sister's son. He had been taken as a British prisoner of war during the encounters in Africa. Similar news filtered through the neighborhood regarding members of other families. The days became long and weary.

Could Cousin Frank be in combat against a relative, I often wondered. Then we learned that Frank fought with the 26th Infantry Division at Casino and Anzio, Italy, and later in France and Germany

"These are the anguishes of war," I heard Papa say to Mama often. We were happy to learn that Peter remained in England as a ground crew member of the Air Force. The pain and sorrow was deeply felt by everyone when news spread about the loss of one of our local men.

During those WWII years, the *Post-Gazette* of Massachusetts and *La Notizia*, both North End newspapers were published in Italian. They provided news to the many immigrants who had never learned to read English. Families waited for mail from Italy, but that was very slow reaching this country during wartime. They searched the Italian newspapers for information about both Americans and those from their homeland.

During the war, a transformation of the area adjacent to the

North End Park took place. The many vacant brick waterfront buildings on Commercial Street, empty for numerous years, became the location of the U.S. Coast Guard Base. The North End residents welcomed the Coast Guard and their personnel to the community.

Each time I walked up Charter Street towards the Copp's Hill Burying Ground and Slye Park, I could see "Old Ironsides" (the frigate *Constitution*) safely docked at the Charlestown Navy Yard. From the North End Park Pier, I remember watching the large destroyers maneuvering in and out of the Navy Yard docks. Traffic along the channel waters of Boston Harbor increased daily. My friends and I went to see the *Wasp* when it docked at the South End Pier. Our friend, Louis had been stationed on the *Wasp* until a serious injury to his leg occurred during a training mission. The sight of the huge battleship left us speechless. It stood taller than the buildings in that area.

I was inspired when a friend invited Mama and me to see a destroyer being launched from the Charlestown Navy Yard. I remember writing to Peter and telling him how Mama and I sat on bleacher-type seat at the Navy Yard with hundreds of people on a chilly fall day. We both shed tears of pride that day. The band played loudly while a lady broke a bottle of champagne on the bow of the destroyer. We stood up with the crowd, clapping and cheering as the ship slowly slid into the Boston Harbor after the christening.

Like all other cities and towns, air-raid shelters developed. Signs appeared at the local schools with instructions on where to go when the alarm sounded. Men and women in the community volunteered to be air-raid wardens.

"Where will we go and what will we do when that air-raid alarm goes off?" I asked as we walked home from school. Then one day it happened. As the alarm bellowed we rushed into a nearby apartment building and huddled together until we heard the loud "all clear" blast penetrate the air.

"At least we don't have bombs falling over us," Mama said to several frightened and frustrated customers who complained about the loud air-raid warnings. I sat quietly, thinking of what Mama said about the terrified people in England who had to endure the bombs destroying their homes and neighborhoods.

Those days taught me that when necessary, one could quickly learn to obey new rules and regulations. Evening air-raid drills were a signal to lower our dark green window shades in our apartment. Each night, to block out any light to outside viewers, Papa lowered the large black window shades in the bakery and one over the glass on the entrance door.

Many families living in the North End seldom traveled out of the neighborhood. But soon everyone became accustomed to servicemen and women traveling by train via North or South Station. For twenty-four hours, the stations were crowded with family members waiting patiently for servicemen or women to arrive, while others waved to those departing.

In 1943, I was invited out to supper with one of my friends whose brother Joe had become a navigator in the U.S. Air Force. It was his last day at home. An older sister realized he might be going overseas soon. After supper, we drove to what was then the small East Boston's Logan Airport. We drove onto the field and stopped about thirty or forty feet from a large Air Force plane. We said our good-byes and saw Joe walk to the plane and climb aboard. We waved as the plane taxied out for take off. My heart pounded as we all watched with teary eyes. I wondered if we would ever see him again. The daylight was fading fast, but we continued waving as our eyes followed the ascending plane until it disappeared into the darkening sky. As time passed during the war, we heard about more planes leaving and landing at Logan, eventually causing the need to enlarge the airport.

After Pearl Harbor, letter writing became an important priority in my life. Papa's earlier conversations on how he yearned for mail when he was in the service prompted me to write often to our many relatives and friends. V-mail made it easy to send Peter daily notes during his stay in England. Before holidays, Mama prepared packages to send to Peter and nephews.

In November 1944, President Franklin Roosevelt became

the only U.S. President ever to be elected to a fourth term. Then our hearts filled with sadness on April 12, 1945, at the death of this President who had successfully guided our country through terrifying years.

Twenty-six days after his death, bells rang gloriously on May 8 from every church steeple, signaling the end of the European War. Hundreds poured into the North End streets and churches in tears and cried, "Thank God."

Three month later, eight days after the bombing of Hiroshima, the Japanese emperor surrendered on August 14, 1945 in Japan. *The church bells rang again for this final victory.*. Once again people erupted into the streets, laughing, crying and hugging each other while dancing together with joy. Adults and children appeared from apartment windows, happily banging metal pan covers together or hitting spoons against their pans in celebration. Mama and I joined the numerous neighbors who went to say a prayer of thanksgiving at St. Stephen's Church.

Slowly our service men and women returned to the community. Some arrived with wives or husbands. Others came to visit family but planned to live elsewhere. Boyfriends and girlfriends finally arranged to be married.

We greeted all the servicemen and women proudly as they returned. In later years, as an expression of gratitude for their years of service during those war years, I remember joining my family and the North End American Legion Post #53 members in making frequent visits to the Chelsea Soldier's Home and Hospital nearby. On Memorial Day, Thanksgiving week and at Christmas time, we volunteered to bring desserts, candy and ice cream to those ill, wounded or disabled in the hospital or living there. On Memorial Day we went to St. Michael's Cemetery in Forrest Hills, Jamaica Plain, to place flags on the graves of servicemen and women.

Music Sheet of Christmas Prayer song written for Christmas
school assembly in 1943.

CHRISTMAS PRAYER

Christmas Day is here again,
Santa's on his way,
Many hearts will be so sad
On that Sacred day.

Our church bells will ring,
And our hearts should sing,
Yet tears will fall in rhythm of
Those beautiful hymns.

Then Santa will drop
Through our chimney top
So many toys for girls and boys
While mothers sit and pray.

Dear Lord whose birthday is today?
Please have those far away
Successfully fill their wondrous tasks
So they'll come home to stay.

Then next year we'll join in
And though with tears we'll sing,
They'll be tears of happiness
If bells of PEACE will ring.

NOTE: In 1943, during my second year at Boston Clerical
School, I had remained a member of the school chorus. Some of
my friends knew that I enjoyed writing poetry and lyrics to music.

I had composed a few songs during high school days. Someone told our chorus instructor. As we neared Christmas that year, she asked if I would try to compose something that the school chorus could sing at Christmas Assembly. The main thought on my mind was the war and all those, including my brother, who was far away from home. I composed music and lyrics to the Christmas Prayer for which the instructor wrote the harmony. The chorus practiced it a few weeks and we happily sang it at the Christmas Assembly.

I stored it away after that day until our servicemen left for the Gulf War. I decided to send it as a poem during the Christmas season to the *Post-Gazette* editor. It has been published three times as a poem in the editor's column of the *Post-Gazette* of Boston.

Part Two

RECIPES FROM THE HOMELAND

A collection of Italian Family Recipes

By

Vita Orlando Sinopoli

Charter Street Press

PART TWO

RECIPES FROM THE HOMELAND

INTRODUCTION

My parents and many of our relatives came to America from Sicily during the Industrial Revolution in the early 1900s. Although they brought only a few possessions, the women carried in their minds the family recipes they learned from their mothers and grandmothers.

Back in their homeland, these families had lived in difficult economic times so women had served simple meals. Most families grew their own grain as tenant farmers or on small-inherited plots of land. They milled grain into flour for their homemade breads and pasta. Vegetables, beans, and legumes were prepared fresh daily or preserved. They raised hens and roosters to supply eggs and poultry meals. Goats supplied them with milk. On special occasions, beef and veal were served.

During religious holidays, villagers gathered in the homes of friends and relatives to prepare special festive dishes and share their bounty. Relatives and neighbors exchanged baked goods. They then attended church services and walked in the town's festival processions with joy and thanksgiving.

When they came to Boston, my parents and their friends continued to celebrate these traditional festivities. I grew up in this atmosphere and learned many of the recipes. As my children grew I enjoyed preparing these meals with them. Today, I also happily prepare many of these meals with grandchildren when they visit my husband and me.

My goal in this book is to share these memories of special occasions along with the recipes, from main meals to deserts, so others may carry on the traditions of our ancestors. I also hope that these recipes will bring a bit of the "Old World" into other lives as well.

Vita Orlando Sinopoli

BREADED EGGPLANT

Baked or fried

1 medium-size eggplant
2 cups prepared bread crumbs
2 beaten eggs
3/4 cup olive, vegetable or canola oil

Remove dark eggplant skin with paring knife or potato peeler. Slice eggplant into one-quarter-inch rounds. Layer slices on a flat dish and salt lightly. Beads of liquid will appear on the slices as they rest one on top of the other. Cover eggplant with wax or plastic paper and place in the refrigerator for at least a half-hour.

FOR FRYING: With paper towels, wipe beads of liquid from each eggplant slice before dipping into beaten eggs. Then coat with prepared bread crumbs and set aside in a platter.

Heat one-quarter cup of oil in a skillet. Place breaded slices in heated oil and fry until brown on both sides. Place fried eggplant slices on paper towels to absorb oil. Then set aside on a clean platter. Because eggplant slices absorb oil while frying, additional oil may be needed in the skillet as you fry.

FOR BAKING: Place breaded eggplant slices on an oiled baking tray. Drip small amount of oil on top of each slice in the tray. Bake in a preheated 350°F oven for fifteen minutes. Turn over all slices that have browned. Return to oven and bake another ten to fifteen minutes. Check often in order not to burn. Remove from oven when browned and tender to your liking. Continue baking remaining breaded eggplant slices in this fashion.

Serve hot or cooled. Remaining cooked eggplant slices can be refrigerated. Reheat in microwave oven for later servings.

Note: Some North End neighbors planted eggplant seeds in large containers on their fire escapes or on the roof. Some grew them in their rented garden lots in Revere or Woburn. Others waited to purchase eggplants in produce stores on Salem, Cross, and Blackstone Streets. Today they are available throughout the year.

When baked, they are a tasty and nutritious snack that can also be served as hors d'oeuvre.

CAPONATA

Eggplant

1 medium eggplant diced
6 or 7 tablespoons olive oil
1 sliced onion
3 tablespoons prepared tomato sauce
2 stalks celery diced
2 tablespoon wine vinegar
1 tablespoon sugar
1 tablespoon capers
4 green pimento olives
1/4 teaspoon salt
1/8 tablespoon ground pepper
A sprinkle of cayenne pepper (optional)

Wash eggplant whole, and dice. Do not remove outer skin. Heat five tablespoons of olive oil in a skillet and add diced eggplant to simmer until it softens. Add sliced onion to skillet and one or two teaspoons of additional olive oil and fry until onion is lightly browned. Add tomato sauce and diced celery. Simmer mixture until celery is tender. If needed, add a tablespoon of water before adding capers and chopped green pimento olives. Stir frequently to prevent sticking.

Slightly heat wine vinegar separately. Add sugar and stir. Then pour wine vinegar gently over eggplant mixture in skillet. Simmer for ten to fifteen minutes. (Optional) Add a sprinkle of cayenne pepper. Salt to taste.

Serve this hot or cooled as a side dish with broiled lamb

chops, breaded fried cutlets or roast beef. It is also delicious on crackers or on toasted bread to serve as hors d'oeuvres.

Caponata can be refrigerated for future servings. It can also be frozen and reheated.

Note: My husband and I met Louis and Rose "Dolly" Sorrentino on Cape Cod in the 1980s. They were former North End neighbors of ours for many years. We renewed our friendships.

While having lunch at their Cape Cod home one day, Dolly served us some homemade Caponata. I mentioned how much I had enjoyed it when my mother served it. But my mother prepared Caponata only during the summer when eggplants were available. Like so many of her friends, Mama never had a written recipe. I was delighted that Dolly offered me a copy of her recipe. Because eggplants are now available year round, we can enjoy homemade Caponata throughout the year.

MAMA'S HOMESTYLE PIZZA

DOUGH:
1 cup lukewarm water
1 package dry yeast*
2 tablespoons oil
1 teaspoon salt
1 teaspoon sugar
2 cups flour
*If using Rapid Rise Highly Active Yeast, follow direction on the package.

PIZZA TOPPINGS:
1 pizza baking tray approx. 14" x 16"
8 ounces shredded mozzarella cheese
14 ounces crushed tomatoes
4 tablespoons Romano grated cheese
3 tablespoons oregano
1/4 cup olive oil or oil of choice
Salt

DOUGH PREPARATION: Place lukewarm water in a bowl. Sprinkle yeast over water and mix until dissolved. Add oil, sugar, salt and stir. Gradually add flour until all water is absorbed. If dough is too soft, add additional flour until it is the desired consistency. Spread a little oil in bowl before placing dough in bowl. Cover with a clean towel and set aside to rise. Put in a warm place. Dough will be ready for spreading when it doubles in size.

PIZZA: Spread some oil over bottom of baking tray. For

ease of spreading dough in tray, moisten both hands with oil. Flatten and spread dough in tray to thickness desired.

TOPPINGS: Sprinkle mozzarella over dough, followed by topping with crushed tomato. Spread grated cheese and oregano over tomato. Sprinkle olive oil over contents and along inside edges of pizza. Other toppings of choice like chopped mushrooms vegetables of choice can be added. Salt to taste. Bake in preheated 400°F oven for about twenty minutes. Thickness of dough and the number of toppings may vary time of baking. Bottom of pizza should brown.

To increase recipe, guideline is one cup of water for two cups of flour, except when using cake flour. When using cake flour, additional flour may be needed for the one cup of water.

Note: It was always a festive time for our children when my parents prepared pizza at home for us. Mama mixed the dough by memory. The children watched Papa add the toppings. After years of watching them at home or in the bakery, I wrote out the ingredients and measurements they used. I have shared this recipe with my children, friends, and relatives. Though prepared dough is readily available now in most supermarkets, I still prefer mixing Mama's pizza dough recipe for our baked-at-home pizza.

POTATO SALAD ALLA ITALIANA

4 potatoes
1 large onion (Vidalia preferred in season)
3 tablespoons olive oil
1 tablespoon oregano
3 tablespoons cider vinegar
Salt and pepper

Peel skins from potatoes. Cut into one and a half or two-inch portions. Wash potatoes and set aside. Heat enough water in a saucepan to a boil. Add potato portions. Cover saucepan. Boil potato portions until tender (about fifteen to twenty minutes). Do not overcook.

While potatoes are cooking, remove outer skin from onion. Cut onion in half, lengthwise, and then into one-quarter-inch strips. Set aside.

Strain potatoes from water when fork tender and place in a bowl. While potato portions are hot, add the onion, olive oil, oregano, cider vinegar, salt and pepper to taste. Mix the contents thoroughly. Cover bowl and place in refrigerator to chill before serving.

Additional vinegar may be added for a more vinegary taste.

OPTIONAL: Potatoes may be washed and placed whole in heated water to boil until skin separates slightly (approximately thirty minutes). Place potatoes in a bowl. Remove skin and then cut and follow directions given above. I find additional flavor from potatoes when boiled whole with skin.

Serves four.

Note: As a youngster, I helped Mama many times as she

prepared large portions of this salad for summer cookouts in Wilmington. This popular potato salad also traveled frequently with us to the numerous family picnics. Aunts, uncles, and cousins gathered in one or two of Papa's trucks and followed us to north or south shore beaches.

This is not only simple to make but can be prepared the previous day. Allowing the potatoes, oil, vinegar and oregano to blend overnight in the refrigerator enhances the flavor of this salad.

SICILIAN GREEN OLIVE SALAD

1 jar Sicilian green olives*
2 stalks celery chopped
1 large onion chopped
1 large garlic clove minced
1 tablespoon oregano
2 tablespoons olive, canola, or vegetable oil
2 tablespoons cider vinegar
Salt

*Sicilian green olives are not usually found pitted. To pit olives, use a paring knife to cut olive meat from olive pit. Another method is to place each olive, one by one, on a cutting board. Using a wooden mallet, hit the olive so that the meat separates and exposes the olive pit. Place olive meat in a large bowl.

Add chopped celery, onion and minced garlic to the olives and mix. Sprinkle oregano, oil and cider vinegar over the mixture and mix thoroughly. Additional oregano, oil, vinegar or salt may be added. When kept in a clean covered jar or bowl this salad stores well for a lengthy time in refrigerator. This salad is ready for serving within thirty minutes of preparation.

Note: In my childhood, I remember my father buying a large wooden box of shinny light green olives from the produce market. The large quantity was to be shared with aunts who lived nearby. The women knew how much water and salt were needed to soak the olives and how long before they could be ready for this special Sicilian salad.

In 1931, when my parents took the family to Sicily to meet our paternal grandmother, my brother Peter and I had the privilege of going to the olive groves with our relatives to harvest olives. As a six-year-old, I thought of it as a picnic day under the beautiful but old craggy-looking olive trees. We ate lunch and stayed most of the day before returning in the horse-drawn carts.

Another day, Papa and his brother-in-law, Uncle Nino, took us to a processing plant near their hometown. There we saw olives that had been crushed, processed and stored in huge containers. The scent of olive oil was so strong in that small, cold processing plant that it made my eyes tear. I wanted to rush out into the fresh air. My love for the green olives and the olive oil extracted from them grew from that experience.

STUFFED GREEN BELL PEPPERS

3 green bell peppers cut lengthwise (six halves)
3 cups cooked rice of choice*
1 pound ground beef
3 eggs
1 tablespoon grated Romano cheese (optional)
1/4 cup olive, canola or vegetable oil
3 cups prepared tomato sauce
Salt

Prepare rice of choice according to direction on the rice package. Set aside.

Cut each pepper in half lengthwise. Remove stem and seeds and wash thoroughly. Set aside and allow drying.

In a bowl, mix cooked rice and ground beef. Add two beaten eggs, salt and pepper to taste.

OPTIONAL: If preferred, ground beef can be lightly browned in skillet to remove excess fat prior to adding beef to the cooked rice.

Add grated cheese to bowl and mix thoroughly. With tablespoon, fill opening of each half-pepper with the rice and beef mixture until all halves have been stuffed. (*Approx. ½ cup cooked rice plus 1 ½ tablespoon of ground beef is used to stuff each half-pepper.)

Beat one egg in a separate bowl. Use pastry brush to spread beaten egg over top of each stuffed pepper.

Heat oil in a skillet. Lower heat before carefully placing three half-peppers (stuffing side down) into the skillet. Fry peppers until stuffing browns slowly. With spatula, turn each half-pepper over gently. Check frequently to avoid burning while frying remaining peppers in this manner

Line bottom baking tray or casserole dish with some prepared tomato sauce. Place fried peppers (stuffing face up) in tray. With tablespoon, spread some tomato sauce over each stuffed pepper. (Optional: Sprinkle grated cheese over each pepper.) Cover and bake in a preheated 350°F oven for about forty minutes. Remove cover and bake until tops brown lightly and peppers are fork tender (approx. ten to twenty additional minutes).

Note: My sister-in-law Rose Sinopoli taught me this recipe many years ago. The stuffed bell peppers became a popular food for family gatherings. My children prepare them frequently in their own homes. Today these bell peppers are available in various colors.

ROASTED (BROILED) RED BELL PEPPERS

4 red peppers
1 large garlic clove minced
3 tablespoons olive oil
Salt
4 brown paper lunch bags

Wash and dry red peppers thoroughly. Place them whole on a broiling tray under the broiler. Broil until the outer skin of pepper begins to darken. Check frequently by removing from oven and turn each pepper as it blackens. It only takes a few minutes for the skin to blacken. (If left under broiler too long, the pepper will burn.) Continue broiling and turning in this fashion until most of the outer skin of each pepper has blackened though not necessarily the entire pepper. Remove peppers from oven.

Put one or two peppers together in a paper lunch bag and close tightly. Because liquid from peppers may seep through bags, place on a cookie sheet. After cooling in paper bag for at least fifteen to thirty minutes, take one bag at a time and place on clean dish. Tear open bag and carefully peel off outer skin of each softened pepper. Gently cut around the stem to remove stem and seeds from the pepper. Cut pepper in half and remove any remaining seeds. Slice pepper into long one-inch strips and set aside in a separate bowl. Liquid will accumulate as pepper strips rest in bowl. Save for marinade.

Spread minced garlic over pepper strips in a bowl. Add olive oil and stir thoroughly. Salt to taste. Cover and place in refrigerator or on your counter. Before serving, to enhance flavor, marinate roasted/broiled peppers at least thirty minutes in the garlic, oil and pepper liquids. The peppers can be heated in the microwave if desired.

They store well, for a few days, in the refrigerator in a clean jar or plastic container.

Note: Because they were only available in the summer when I was young, I welcome the opportunity to prepare them often now that peppers can be purchased daily. My family enjoys them with baked chicken, steaks, or chops.

VINE-RIPENED TOMATO SALAD

3 vine-ripened tomatoes
1 large cucumber
1 large onion
3 tablespoons oregano
3 tablespoons virgin olive oil
Salt and black pepper

Wash tomatoes thoroughly. Cut each tomato lengthwise into quarters. Cut each quarter into one-inch portions. Place in serving bowl. Then remove outer skin from cucumber and slice thinly as for salad. Add to tomatoes. Remove skin from onion. Wash and cut in half, lengthwise. Slice halves into 1/3-long slices. Add to tomatoes and cucumber slices. Sprinkle oregano and virgin olive oil over contents in the bowl. Add salt and pepper to taste. Mix thoroughly before serving.

The combination of vine-ripened tomatoes and virgin olive oil enhances the flavor of this salad though regular olive oil, canola or vegetable oil can be used.

Note: When I prepare this vine-ripened tomato salad today, I often think about growing up in Boston's North End. Fresh vine-ripened tomatoes were only available for sale during mid-summer. However, from springtime to fall, during those depression days, we experienced the sight and fragrances of "container gardens" resting on our fire escapes and roof areas. My friends and I saw tomatoes grow from the small yellow blossoms that appeared on the tomato plants in these containers.

Some North Enders rented gardening lots in Revere or Woburn to grow their tomatoes, vegetables and herbs. I waited patiently for tomatoes and cucumbers to be harvested from my parent's garden lot in Silver Lake, Wilmington, MA.

Mama served us the fresh tomato salad for lunch many times together with our fresh bread, some cheese and roasted black olives. We also enjoyed the salad with suppers of baked poultry or meats.

VINEGAR (PICKLED) PEPPERS

1 quart white vinegar
1 quart water
5 green bell peppers
3 medium pickling jars with screw caps.
3 teaspoons salt
3 teaspoons sugar

Place white vinegar and water in a saucepan over medium heat and cover. Bring to a rolling boil for about three minutes.

Meanwhile remove stems and seeds from peppers. Wash peppers thoroughly. Cut peppers into quarter portions lengthwise and place in clean jars. Pour enough boiled water and vinegar combination over peppers, up to rim of jar. Add one teaspoon of salt and one teaspoon of sugar to each jar. Place cover tightly on each jar.

On a clean cookie sheet or cutting board, turn closed jar upside down, resting jar on its cover. Check to be sure that water is not leaking from jar. Allow standing for thirty minutes before turning jars right side up. Store for three or four weeks in you cupboard before use. Refrigerate only after opening jars.

Note: I began to pickle bell peppers in the 1950s when my cousin Josie (LaGrassa) DeSisto shared her recipe with me. Each time I pickled peppers, my mind wandered back to my childhood when each fall, Papa bought a case of the small Santo Nicolo peppers for pickling. They were small but firm. They were green, and some were spotted with a little red, or yellow skin. While Mama washed the peppers without removing stem or inner seeds, Papa prepared the very large ceramic container. It was the same kind that everyone else in the neighborhood used for pickling peppers.

After the peppers were clean, my parents placed them in the container and added the necessary vinegar and spices. I remember Papa placing a large ceramic cover on the container. He warned us not to go near the peppers.

All this took place in the little cubical of space in the cellar of 39 Charter Street, below our bakery. Each family had a cubical reserved for storing extra canned goods, wine, and preserved vegetables. Before long, the aroma of the pickled peppers found its way up to the street floor of the building. Papa wasn't the only one who had pickled peppers.

Each time I look at the ceramic container, still in my possession, it reminds me of the above yearly ritual.

BAKED SCALLOPS

1 pound scallops
25 Ritz-or Hi-Ho-type crackers crushed
1 tablespoon chopped parsley
2 tablespoons butter or margarine
2 tablespoons white wine
Paprika
Salt

Spread some butter or margarine at bottom of baking dish (10" x 12" x 2"). Wash scallops and drain excess water. Place scallops in baking dish. Blend melted butter into cracker crumbs. *Spread crumbs over scallops. Pour two tablespoons of white wine in a glass with two tablespoons of clam juice or water. Sprinkle gently over cracker crumbs and scallops. Sprinkle paprika over the cracker crumbs. Cover and bake at 400°F for fifteen or twenty minutes or until scallops are the right consistency to serve.

*Note: *When preparing the above recipe for my husband and me, I sprinkle garlic powder over the scallops before adding the cracker crumbs and remaining ingredient. We enjoy the garlic flavoring.*

I often bake this meal in my heated toaster oven set on broil. I cover scallops with aluminum foil before placing in toaster oven. Broil for about eight to ten minutes. Then set the toaster oven to bake for the remaining time needed.

I serve mashed potatoes or rice pilaf along with French-cut beans and/or carrot strips topped with butter or margarine.

BROILED OR BAKED HADDOCK ALLA SICILIANA

Broiled Haddock Sicilian Style

1 pound haddock fillet
1 medium onion
1 large chopped garlic clove or garlic powder
2 fresh tomatoes
1 tablespoon oregano flakes
1 or 2 tablespoons grated Romano cheese (optional)
2 tablespoons olive, canola, or vegetable oil
Salt and pepper

Spread some oil on bottom of a broiling tray or baking pan. Place haddock fillet skin down on tray or baking pan. Cut tomatoes into ¼-inch slices and place over haddock fillet. Cut onion in ¼-inch slices and layer over tomato. Sprinkle oregano, salt and pepper to taste over onion. Spread chopped garlic, or garlic powder, over contents. (Optional) sprinkle grated cheese over contents. Next, sprinkle oil of choice over all. Cover and place at least two inches below broiling coils. Broil for about fifteen minutes. Remove from broiler. If dry, add a small amount of water. Cover and return to broil for about ten minutes. Remove from oven. Baste haddock with the liquids that accumulate in the broiling tray or baking pan. Return uncovered and brown onions and tomato. Check frequently to prevent burning or drying out.

*Cooking time for the haddock fillet depends on the thickness of the fillet.

Note: When Mama prepared this meal, I remember enjoying the fragrances of garlic, tomato, oregano and broiling fish that spread throughout the kitchen. Mama liked adding some Romano grated cheese occasionally over the contents. She referred to this meal as "Haddock alla Pizzaiola."

As the haddock cooked, I checked to be sure that we had plenty of bread available at home. I enjoyed dunking my bread in the juices while eating the broiled fish, and I still do.

CALAMARI IMBOTTITI

Stuffed Squid

2 pounds squid (calamari, already cleaned)
20 crushed Hi-Ho-or Ritz-type crackers
3 tablespoons softened butter or margarine
Paprika (optional)

With a knife or scissors, separate tentacles from each calamari. Cut tentacles into one-inch portions. Wash calamari and tentacles separately and drain before placing in separate bowls.

STUFFING: In another bowl, crush crackers, add softened butter or margarine of choice and blend into cracker crumbs. Add tentacle portions, mix thoroughly, and set aside.

Line bottom of a 9" x 9" baking dish with vegetable spray or butter.

Using a teaspoon, fill the calamari cavity **halfway** with stuffing mixture. Place stuffed calamari side by side in baking dish. Spread any remaining stuffing mixture over them. Top calamari with a dab of margarine or butter. Cover and bake in a preheated 375°F oven for about twenty to twenty-five minutes or until fork tender. They will shrink in size as they bake.

OPTIONAL: Sprinkle paprika lightly over calamari prior to baking.

Note: Mama pleased us with many different Calamari recipes during the year, particularly in Lent. I continue to prepare this recipe for my family. We especially savor succulent stuffed squid on Christmas and New Year's Eve.

CALAMARI (SQUID) IN TOMATO SAUCE OVER LINGUINE

14 ounces crushed tomatoes
1 medium chopped onion
1 large chopped garlic clove (optional)
¼ cup olive, canola or vegetable oil
1 teaspoon dried basil or two fresh basil leaves
2 pounds already cleaned calamari (squid)
3 tablespoons white or red wine of choice
1 pound of linguine
Grated Romano or Parmesan cheese

Heat oil in skillet, add chopped onion, garlic (optional), and basil. Simmer until onion is opaque. Garlic should not brown. Add crushed tomatoes and stir thoroughly. Cover and simmer sauce until it comes to a slow boil. Lower heat and simmer for about twenty minutes. Stir occasionally to prevent sauce from sticking to the bottom of skillet. If mixture appears to be too thick, add a half-cup of water and stir.

Cut tentacles from calamari if not already separated. Wash and cut each calamari into approximately one-inch widths. Do not cut lengthwise. A small calamari should give about three portions. Wash both thoroughly. Set aside in a bowl.

When sauce has simmered about twenty minutes, add calamari and tentacles. Then stir and cover. Simmer calamari in sauce for about five minutes. Do not over cook. calamari will become tough if cooked too long. Cover and remove skillet from heat until you are ready to cook pasta.

Cook linguine, or pasta of your choice, according to the directions on the package.

While pasta is cooking, return calamari sauce mixture to burner to reheat slowly. Add three tablespoons of red or white wine of choice. Bring to a slow boil. Turn off burner and remove from heat. Place cooked and strained pasta onto a serving platter and top with tomato sauce, calamari, and grated cheese of choice.

OPTIONAL: Adding additional calamari to the sauce will allow some to be served with the pasta and some separately with a fresh green salad. Remaining sauce freezes well.

Serves two.

Note: In the 1930s, I remember my mother standing at the sink removing the thin layer of outer skin and the inner portions of the squid. She removed the tentacles and placed them in a separate bowl. When I asked if she was throwing the tentacles away she quickly replied. " No! Sono buoni!" (They are good!) Mama was right. I always include them in the sauce.

LINGUINE WITH CLAMS IN BIANCO

In White Sauce

2 dozen freshly steamed littleneck clams*
4 or 5 garlic cloves chopped
1/4 cup of olive, canola oil, or a mixture of both
1 tablespoon chopped parsley (preferable fresh)
Romano or Parmesan grated cheese
1 pound linguine

OPTIONAL: In place of freshly steamed clams, use two cans of chopped or minced clams and two bottles of clam juice available in supermarkets.

To steam clams: Wash clam shells thoroughly several times. Add about one quarter of an inch of water to saucepan and place on burner to heat. Then add clams. Cover and allow steaming until the clamshells open. Remove saucepan from burner. Remove clams from shells and set aside. Save the broth.

White sauce preparation: Skin and chop garlic cloves. Heat oil slightly in two-quart saucepan over medium heat before adding chopped garlic. Simmer slowly. Do not brown garlic. Remove pan from burner for a few seconds before adding parsley and clam broth from steamed clams. Return to burner and bring to a boil. Add clams, chopped or whole. When mixture comes to a boil, turn off burner. Cover and let stand.

Follow directions on package for cooking linguine or pasta as desired. After draining cooked pasta in colander, place in serving bowl. Pour clam broth from saucepan over linguine. Top each serving with one or more tablespoons of clams. Serve with preferred grated cheese.

Use directions above for preparing oil, garlic mixture. Remove saucepan from burner and let stand a few seconds before adding parsley, bottled clam juice and clams. Bring to a slow boil for a few seconds. Turn off burner. Cover and let stand. Then follow directions above for serving the clams in bianco with the cooked pasta.

Serves four.

Note: One of my delights is to prepare this meal for my family and friends with fresh steamed littlenecks whenever possible. It always reminds me of the many times we experienced the pleasure of digging for littlenecks along various north or south shore beaches during my childhood. We couldn't wait to return home for Mama to prepare this meal for us.

Whenever I use fresh steamed littlenecks today, I make sure to save some in the shell after steaming. I top each serving bowl of linguine with the chopped littlenecks and a few littlenecks in the shell.

NONNA MARY'S FISH CAKES

1 pound of cod or haddock fillet
3 large or 4 small potatoes
1 tablespoon grated Romano cheese
2 tablespoons chopped parsley
2 1/2 tablespoons butter or margarine
1 egg beaten
1 four-quart pan
Medium-size Teflon skillet
1/4 cup cooking oil
l/4 cup dried bread crumbs (optional)

Peel, cut and wash potatoes. Cover potatoes with water in the four-quart pan and bring to a boil. Boil for fifteen minutes. Meanwhile remove all skin and bones from fish. Add cleaned fish to boiling potatoes. (If desired, fish may be boiled separately). Boil fish and potatoes slowly for about ten to twelve minutes. When potatoes and fish are cooked, drain contents in colander for a few minutes. While still warm, place potatoes and fish in a bowl with butter and salt to taste. Add grated Romano cheese, parsley, and beaten egg. Stir and mix well. If mixture is too soft, add some bread crumbs to absorb any extra liquid. Store covered in refrigerator to cool. Mixture is easier to shape into flat fish cakes when cool.

SHAPING: Take a FULL tablespoon of mixture in hand and shape like a flattened meatball. Heat oil in skillet. Fry fish cakes until golden brown. Turn over with spatula to brown on other side. Then remove from skillet and place in paper plate to absorb excess oil.

OPTIONAL: For those who prefer baked food, place the fish cake mixture in a lightly oil-sprayed baking dish. After covering the baking dish with aluminum foil, place it in a preheated 350°F oven to bake for about twenty minutes. Remove cover to lightly brown top before serving.

Serve with vegetable of choice or salad.

Note: This is a recipe taught to me by my mother-in-law, Mary Sinopoli. It has been a long-time favorite of the family. I often receive requests today from our children and grandchildren for the fried fish cakes. It takes a little patience to fry them, but my pleasure is in seeing everyone enjoying them. Some prefer the baked mixture so I usually make some of each.

PESCE STOCCO

"Stock Fish"
Cod or Haddock in Tomato Sauce

1 pound codfish loins
1 medium chopped onion
3 small potatoes
1 celery stick (chopped)
1 bay leaf (optional)
3 medium-ripe tomatoes, or
1 four-ounce can tomato sauce
1/4 cup olive or canola oil
2 tablespoons capers in vinegar
2 tablespoons white wine
Salt

Peel and chop onion and celery. Place cooking oil, onion and celery in skillet to simmer slowly until onion is opaque. Add capers including some of the liquid from bottle and stir. Simmer slowly. Add chopped fresh tomatoes, cover and simmer a few minutes. Add bay leaf (optional). If used, be sure to remove bay leaf before serving meal. Allow ingredients to cook about ten minutes being careful not to dry them out.

Peel, wash, and cut potatoes into two-inch wedges. Add to skillet. Spoon some tomato sauces from skillet over potatoes. Cover and simmer slowly, about ten to twelve minutes. Rinse cod loins. Cut into four-inch pieces before adding to skillet. Add water if needed to extend sauce. Spoon some sauce over the cod pieces. Cover and cook slowly. When fish and potatoes is fork tender, add wine and bring to slow boil. Cover and remove from burner. Reheat slowly for serving.

Note: During the mid-eighteen hundreds, my ancestors in Sicily prepared this as a special Christmas Eve meal. My parents and relatives continued the tradition in this country. Two or three days before preparing this recipe, the dried pesce stocco (which I believe to be dried cured haddock) was soaked in water. The water was changed daily to remove the salt. However, the briny taste remained. This was not a popular meal with many young children because of the strong unpleasant aroma while the fish cooked. But eventually it became a favorite meal served with fresh bread.

Since dried salted haddock is difficult to find today, fresh or dried salted cod (baccala) can be used instead. When I prepare the meal now, I use fresh skinned cod loins, free of bones. This eliminates the unpleasant aroma of the preserved fish. To obtain the "old briny" taste, I add two small pieces of presoaked dried, cured baccala.

ROLLED GREY SOLE FILLET

With Rice and Shrimp Stuffing

6 grey sole fillet*
1/4 pound medium Shrimp
20-25 Ritz or Hi Ho crackers
2 tablespoons butter or margarine
1 tablespoon mayonnaise
3 tablespoons white wine
1/2 cup water or clam juice
3/4 cup rice of choice
*Fillet of flounder can be used in place of grey sole fillet.

Cook rice according to directions on the package. Set aside.
Peel shrimp and place in a bowl with water and set aside.

Crush crackers thoroughly. Add softened butter or margarine and work it into crushed crackers. Set aside.

Drain shrimp. On a cutting board, cut up each shrimp into half-inch portions and set aside.

Line bottom of a baking casserole dish lightly with mayonnaise. Spread cooked rice over bottom of casserole.

Wash out the grey sole fillet and drain. Using one fillet at a time, spread some cracker stuffing mixture in center portion of fillet. Add shrimp portions over the stuffing. Starting at narrow edge of fillet, roll the fillet carefully toward the wider end to create the stuffed roll. Continue stuffing remaining fillet. Place each rolled fillet, side by side, over rice in baking dish. With butter knife, spread some mayonnaise lightly over each fillet roll.

Sprinkle some cracker mixture over them and top each roll with 1/8 teaspoon of butter or margarine.

In a cup, mix three tablespoons of white wine in one-half cup of water or clam juice. Spread mixture over rice and rolled fillet.

Place casserole dish in a preheated 375°F oven to bake for fifteen or twenty minutes. Then remove baking dish from oven. Additional water or clam juice can be added to casserole if needed. Return to oven to bake until tops of fillet brown lightly and rolled fillet is fork tender (approx. five to eight minutes).

Note: Watching my elders become creative with foods through the years encouraged me to do the same in my home. This recipe resulted from my curiosity to prepare something different for my family with rice and grey sole fillet. During the summer months, I prepare and bake this recipe in a throwaway aluminum baking dish over low heat on my gas grill.

SALMON STEAKS
BROILED OR GRILLED

4 salmon steaks
2 medium onions
1/4 cup olive, canola or vegetable oil
2 tablespoons mayonnaise
1/4 cup lemon juice
1 teaspoon cider vinegar (optional)
2 tablespoons of butter or margarine

SALMON STEAK: Spread some oil or mayonnaise on the bottom of a broiling pan. Then spread a little oil or mayonnaise over the top and bottom of each salmon steak before placing in the broiling pan. Place in preheated oven about two inches from broiling unit. Turn steaks to broil on both sides slowly. Steaks will turn whitish in color when they are cooked. Depending on size, broiling time will be about fifteen to twenty minutes. Then set broiling pan with steaks aside.

ONIONS: Remove outer skin from onions. Cut onions in half, lengthwise, and then into 1/4-inch slices lengthwise. Set aside in a bowl.

Heat oil in a skillet. Add butter or margarine and onion slices to the skillet. Stir and simmer until onions are about to brown *slightly*. Remove from burner and add lemon juice. Add vinegar (optional). Stir and return to burner. Simmer slowly a few seconds. Remove from burner.

Spoon onions and liquids from skillet over each salmon steak in the broiling pan. Cover with aluminum foil and return to heated broiler for about a minute. To slightly brown tops, remove cover and broil for a few seconds longer.

Serve each steak topped with onions and liquids from broiling pan. Serve with rice pilaf and vegetable or salad of choice. Serves four.

Note: My mother-in-law, Mary Sinopoli, told me often about how she loved to grill her fish or beefsteaks over the hot coals of her Glenwood kitchen stove. From her I learned to try salmon steaks grilled during the summer over our gas-burning grill. I spread a little oil over each steak before grilling both sides of the salmon.

I use my mother's old heavy aluminum skillet over our grill to prepare my onions, oil, and butter and lemon juice mixture. We do experience a different flavor by preparing this recipe in this manner. Either way, this is an enjoyable and easy meal to prepare.

SHRIMP SCAMPI OVER LINGUINE

Or as Hors d'oeuvres

1 pound medium shrimp (cleaned and deveined)
5 cloves chopped garlic
3 tablespoons margarine or butter
2 tablespoons olive oil
2 tablespoons chopped parsley
1 bottle clam juice
1/4 cup white wine or sherry
1 pound linguine
Grated Romano or Parmesan cheese

In a skillet, over low heat, melt margarine or butter and add olive oil. Add chopped garlic. Simmer slowly, careful not to brown garlic. Remove skillet from heat. Slowly add clam juice. Return to heat and add cleaned shrimp. Stir and cover to simmer slowly until all shrimp turn pink (about ten to fifteen minutes). Add wine or sherry and parsley to this broth and cover. Simmer to a boil and then remove from heat. Set aside. Reheat if necessary before serving.

For cooking linguine, follow directions on the package. When pasta is cooked, strain and place pasta in a large serving bowl. Add shrimp broth and stir. Serve linguine in individual bowls topped with shrimp and grated cheese of choice. Place additional broth and shrimp on table for guests.

OPTIONAL: To serve as hors d'oeuvres: Prepare shrimp as mentioned above. Place the prepared Shrimp Scampi in a serving bowl on your table, adding a serving spoon for the guests to help themselves. Also have available plates, forks, and napkins. Garlic bread and/or crackers go well with the hors d'oeuvre.

Note: This easy-to-prepare recipe is one of my brother Peter's specialties that became a favorite in my home. In the 1950s and 60s Peter developed great enthusiasm for cooking. That is when I learned to prepare his Shrimp Scampi. I believe Peter and I inherited Mama's eagerness and joy to try new recipes, hoping always to please the appetite of family and friends.

SHRIMP IN TOMATO SAUCE
OVER LINGUINE

14 ounces of crushed tomatoes
1 medium chopped onion
1 large garlic clove chopped (optional)
1/4 cup olive, canola or vegetable oil
1 teaspoon of dried basil or two fresh basil leaves
1/2 pound fresh medium shrimp
3 tablespoons white wine
Grated cheese of choice

Heat oil in skillet, add chopped onion, garlic (optional), and basil. Simmer until onion is opaque. Garlic should not brown. Add crushed tomatoes and stir thoroughly. Cover and allow the sauce to come to a slow boil. Lower heat and simmer for about twenty minutes. Stir occasionally to prevent sauce from sticking to the bottom of skillet. Add a half-cup of water if mixture appears to be too thick.

Remove outer skin from shrimp. Wash thoroughly and set cleaned shrimp aside in a bowl. When sauce has cooked about twenty minutes, add shrimp, stir and cover. Cook shrimp in sauce until they are pink. Do not over cook shrimp. Cover and remove skillet from heat.

Cook linguine, or pasta of your choice according to the directions on the package. While pasta is cooking, return shrimp-sauce mixture to burner to reheat **slowly**. After a minute, add three tablespoons of white wine to shrimp-sauce mixture. Stir and bring to a *slow* boil. Turn off burner and remove from heat.

When pasta is cooked and strained, place in a serving platter and top with tomato sauce and shrimp.

OPTIONAL: Adding additional shrimp will give enough shrimp to serve with the pasta and some separately with a fresh green salad. Remaining sauce freezes well.

Serves two.

Note: When I was a child, Mama prepared this quick and easy meal often during the Lenten season. Because my husband and I enjoy shrimp, I serve this meal frequently throughout the year. In the summer, I use an older sturdy skillet and prepare this sauce with shrimp on my gas-charcoal grill.

SHRIMP AND SALMON IN BIANCO OVER LINGUINE

(In White Sauce)

4 tablespoons butter or margarine
4 tablespoons olive oil
4 cloves of chopped garlic
1/2 pound medium shrimp
1/2 pound salmon
1 pound linguine
2 bottles clam juice
1 tablespoon chopped parsley
1 tablespoon chopped chives
3 tablespoons white wine
Salt
Romano or Parmesan grated cheese

Remove any skin from salmon steak. Cut up into one-inch portions. Wash and set aside. Remove skin and wash shrimp. Set aside in a separate bowl. In a skillet, soften butter and then add oil to heat. Add chopped garlic and simmer for a few seconds. Do not brown garlic. Lower heat. Add salmon pieces and toss until all pieces begin to whiten. Then add shrimp and toss until all shrimp turn pink. Remove from heat. Add clam juice, parsley, and chives to shrimp and salmon. When mixture comes to a boil, add wine. Bring to a slow boil again. Then remove from burner. Cover and set aside.

Cook linguine according to directions on the package. When pasta is almost cooked, add chopped chives to shrimp and salmon mixture and begin to heat on a separate burner. After straining pasta, place into a serving platter or bowl and add shrimp and salmon broth from saucepan. Top each serving with shrimp and salmon pieces. Serve with preferred grated cheese.

Serves four.

Note: In the past, we have enjoyed littleneck clams with linguine in our home, but occasionally I change the recipe slightly. I use salmon and shrimp in place of littleneck clams. I add butter to the recipe along with some chives and wine for a different flavor.

This is served with warm garlic bread, a fresh green salad, and white wine.

SWORDFISH ALLA MESSINESE

Swordfish Messina Style in Tomato Sauce

1 swordfish steak (about 1 1/4 pounds)
1 medium onion chopped
2 celery stalks chopped
3 teaspoons capers in vinegar and water
3 fresh ripe tomatoes chopped or 10 ounces crushed tomato
2 sprigs bay leaf
3 small potatoes cut in quarters
1/4 cup olive, canola or vegetable oil
1 cup water
2 tablespoons white wine (optional)

Heat oil in a skillet and add chopped onion, chopped celery stalks and simmer until onion is opaque. Add capers, stir, and simmer slowly. Do not brown onion. Add tomato and cover. Cook *slowly* for about five minutes. Check frequently. A little water can be added to keep mixture from sticking to skillet.

Meanwhile, peel and cut potatoes into quarters. Wash and set aside. Rinse swordfish under running water and dry. Cut swordfish into two-inch portions. It is not necessary to remove outer skin of swordfish. Add potatoes first to skillet; add half a cup of water and cover. Allow cooking for about ten minutes. Then add swordfish pieces to skillet. The swordfish can be placed on top of potatoes if skillet becomes crowded. Spoon some of the tomato sauce over the swordfish. Add only small amounts of water if needed after a few minutes. Cover and simmer slowly for about ten to fifteen minutes or until swordfish is fork tender.

Try not to overcook swordfish. Add wine (optional), cover and bring to a slow boil. Then remove from burner.

Serve with fresh Italian bread, vegetable of choice or salad. Serves two.

Variation: Prepare the swordfish recipe without potatoes. Instead, cook rice or pasta of choice as directed on the package and serve topped with the tomato sauce from the skillet. Serve the swordfish separately with vegetable of choice or salad and Italian bread.

Note: Each time I prepare this swordfish meal, I picture my mother-in-law, Mary Sinopoli, at the kitchen stove in our Battery Street apartment. As she carefully prepared the ingredients, she stated, "Swordfish should not be cooked too much as it becomes dry and loses its flavor." I found that to be very true.

In recent years, I have varied this on occasion for my pasta-loving husband by substituting pasta for potatoes as mentioned above.

SWORDFISH STEAKS

Broiled or Grilled

4 swordfish steaks
2 medium onions
1/4 cup olive, canola or vegetable oil
2 tablespoons mayonnaise
1/4 cup lemon juice
1 teaspoon cider vinegar (optional)
2 tablespoons of butter or margarine

SWORDFISH STEAK: Spread some oil or mayonnaise on the bottom of a broiling pan. Then spread a little oil or mayonnaise over the top and bottom of each swordfish steak before placing in the broiling pan. Place in preheated oven about two inches from broiling unit. Turn steaks to broil on both sides slowly. Steaks will turn whitish in color when they are cooked. Depending on size, broiling time will be about fifteen to twenty minutes. Then set broiling pan with steaks aside.

ONIONS: Remove outer skin from onions. Cut onions in half, lengthwise, and then into 1/4-inch slices lengthwise. Set aside in a bowl.

Heat oil in a skillet. Add butter or margarine and onion slices to the skillet. Stir and simmer until onions are about to brown *slightly*. Remove from burner and add lemon juice. Add vinegar (optional). Stir and return to burner. Simmer slowly a few seconds. Remove from burner.

Spoon onions and liquids from skillet over each swordfish steak in the broiling pan. Cover with aluminum foil and return to heated broiler for about a minute. If you desire to brown tops, remove cover and broil for a few seconds longer. Serve each steak topped with onions and liquids from broiling pan. Serves four.

Note: With swordfish available year-round today, I alternate with broiling salmon one time and swordfish the next time. Both are very nutritious and easily prepared in the oven broiler or on a gas or charcoal grill.

BAKED MANICOTTI

In Tomato Sauce with Meat

4 eggs
2 cups flour
2 cups milk
Pinch of salt
2 tablespoons olive or vegetable oil
1 small six-inch cast iron or a non-stick skillet

Practice is needed to be sure the same amount of mixture is poured into skillet for the same size manicotti.

Break eggs into a bowl and beat eggs. Slowly add remaining ingredients one at a time to the bowl. Use an electric mixture on slow speed until it resembles a prepared pancake mix.

Rub inside of cast iron or non-stick skillet with some oil. Heat skillet over burner until it is hot. Remove from heat and with a small ladle, drop about two tablespoons of mixture at one end of skillet. Quickly tip skillet to allow batter to spread over the entire bottom. When firm but not browned (about five seconds), remove by lifting round edge with a fork or small spatula. Place in a dish to cool. There should be no need to turn the round over for further cooking. If you do, be sure not to brown the round crepe. Layer eight or ten prepared rounds one on top of the other. Continue making these until all mixture is used. Stir mixture occasionally.

FILLING:
2 pounds ricotta cheese
2 beaten eggs
Pinch of salt
Pinch of black ground pepper (optional)
3 tablespoons grated cheese of choice (optional)

In a strainer, remove any excess water from ricotta cheese. Then place in a bowl. Add beaten eggs, salt, pepper and grated cheese of choice if desired. Blend but do not whip with electric mixer.

Taking one Manicotti round at a time, place one to two tablespoon of filling in center. Then fold one end of round over the filling. Take opposite end of round and fold over to seal the filling in the stuffed Manicotti.

Using prepared tomato sauce, cover bottom of a Manicotti baking tray with the sauce. Line bottom of baking tray with rows of stuffed Manicotti (seal side down). Spread tomato sauce over them and then sprinkle grating cheese of choice over sauce. A second layer of Manicotti can be placed over the first layer, or if preferred you can continue the process by using another baking tray.

Bake in preheated 400°F degree oven for twenty minutes. Check to see if ricotta mixture needs to bake longer before removing from oven. Ricotta is cooked when you pierce the Manicotti with a toothpick and it comes out clean.

Serves six.

Manicotti rounds can be frozen. Wrap cooled Manicotti in wax paper in groups of eight or ten. Place in seal-locked plastic bags. Wrap each bag in aluminum foil before freezing. To defrost, remove from freezer and then from wrappings. Prepare a large serving tray with a clean towel. Cover with wax paper and allow defrosting on the towel before stuffing.

BEEF HONEYCOMB TRIPE

In Tomato Sauce

TRIPE:
4 to 5 pounds beef honeycomb tripe
2 small onions
5 small dried sprigs bay leaf

TOMATO SAUCE:
14 ounces crushed tomatoes
1 medium onion chopped
1/4 cup olive oil
3 small dried sprigs bay leaf
1 tablespoon basil flakes
1/4 cup red wine
Light sprinkle red pepper flakes (optional)
Salt and pepper

SAUCE:
In an eight-quart pot, heat olive oil over medium heat. Add chopped onion, bay leaf and basil. Simmer slowly, careful not to burn onion. When onion is opaque, add crushed tomatoes and eight ounces of water. Stir thoroughly and cover. Simmer sauce over low/medium heat for about half an hour before adding any tripe. *

TRIPE:
Using an eight-quart pot halfway with cold water. Add peeled whole onions and five small sprigs of bay leaf to pot. Place on burner to boil. When water boils carefully place washed tripe

into the water. Cover and boil moderately for about one hour. (One hour is satisfactory for the first boil of four to five pounds of tripe). Check frequently. Covered pot tends to boil over easily. When tripe is tender but not fully cooked, drain from pot. Add cold water to that pot and place tripe into water.

Drain a portion from the cold water and place on a cutting board. Cut tripe portion into long three-inch strips with sharp knife or scissors. Then cut each three-inch strip diagonally into half-inch-wide portions. Place all cut tripe into separate bowl. After all tripe is cut, run under cold water, drain, and set aside.

*When tomato sauce has cooked about half an hour, add cut-up tripe, salt and a few red pepper flakes (optional). Stir thoroughly. Cover pot and simmer tripe for one hour or until it is tender. (Approx. time—an additional hour). Then add red wine, a sprinkle of red pepper flakes (optional), stir and simmer for one minute before removing from burner.

The tripe and sauce mixture can be reheated before serving. Serves five.

Note: My introduction to tripe was in 1950 when I began preparing this for our Somerville luncheonette customers. I had learned the recipe from watching my mother-in-law, Mary Sinopoli prepare this meal at home. At that time she had to scrape and clean the tripe before boiling it. Today the Tripe is made available already cleaned. This eliminates some of the unpleasant odor and work.

Often times I prepare a double recipe of tripe with tomato sauce and enjoy sharing it with family and friends.

BRACCIOLETINI

20 thin slices of beef (approx. 4" x 4")
1 cup flavored bread crumbs
2 small garlic cloves chopped
1 tablespoon grated Romano cheese
1 tablespoon olive oil
3 metal skewers (6 or 9 inches long)

MARINADE:
1 crushed garlic clove
1 tablespoon dried basil
2 tablespoons olive oil.

Prepare marinade first by mixing crushed garlic clove, basil and olive oil in a bowl and set aside. Then mix bread crumbs, chopped garlic, and grated cheese in a separate bowl. Additional bread crumbs may be needed depending on the number of Braccioletini you prepare. Add olive oil to slightly moisten the bread crumbs. Take one beef slice at a time. Spread about one teaspoon of bread crumbs in the center of meat. Leave sides of meat about half-inch clear of bread crumbs. Gently roll while folding in edges forming a small rolled piece. Squeeze the rolled meat in your hands. Insert metal skewer. Add each rolled Braccioletini onto skewer. They should fit tightly up against each other. When all Braccioletini are on skewers, place them into the marinade. Marinate for about 20 minutes. Before broiling, brush extra marinade over Braccioletini after placing them on the broiling tray. Brown on both sides. Check frequently because they cook fast.

Serve hot with mashed or baked potato and a vegetable or salad.

Note: When I make Braccioletini today, I select a bottom round roast at the supermarket and ask at the deli counter to have it sliced the thickness of cold cuts. Then I cut the larger slices to the size I need. Patience and experience are required but it is well worth the effort.

Braccioletini can be cooked on the gas grill but must be watched because they burn easily.

BRACCIOLI

Served in Tomato Sauce

4 thinly sliced beef steaks
3/4 cup flavored bread crumbs
1 small garlic clove chopped
1 tablespoon of grated Romano cheese
1 tablespoon olive oil
White thread

In a bowl, mix bread crumbs, chopped garlic and grated cheese. Add olive oil to slightly moisten the bread crumbs. Take one beef slice at a time. Spread some bread crumbs in the center of meat. Leave sides of meat about half-inch clear of bread crumbs. Gently roll from long end of meat, gradually folding in the sides so bread crumbs won't fall out. Roll the meat to the end. Squeeze the rolled meat in your hands. Take white thread, and wrap around the roll and sides of meat to secure ends from opening.

Brown on all sides in a skillet before adding to your tomato sauce. Cook in sauce about 45 minutes. Before serving, remove Braccioli from sauce. Let stand in platter a minute before removing thread. Then slice into 1/2-inch portions and serve separately or with cooked pasta.

Note: I learned to make Braccioli from watching my mother and mother-in-law. Patience and experience are needed but are well worth the effort.

In my childhood, I remember going to Moscardino's Meat Market on Salem Street. The butcher cut the beef for Braccioli for the customer as we watched. Today, supermarkets have taken the place of personal butcher shops in many cities. We depend on finding thinly cut beef steaks packaged and on display. Occasionally I have purchased a bottom of the round roast and carefully sliced thin steaks myself to make my Braccioli.

BREADED CUTLETS

2 pounds thinly sliced meat* (approx. 1/4-inch in thickness)
(*Use veal, chicken breast, chicken tenders, turkey breast, or sliced beef)
2 cups flavored bread crumbs
1 or 2 beaten eggs
1/2 cup of olive, canola or vegetable oil
3 paper plates

Place prepared bread crumbs in a bowl. Beat eggs in a separate bowl. With a fork, dip a slice of meat of choice into the beaten egg. Then place it in the bread crumbs. Thoroughly cover both sides of meat with bread crumbs. Place breaded meat in a separate plate. Continue in this fashion until all meat slices are breaded.

Heat one-quarter cup of oil in a skillet. Carefully place breaded meat slices in heated oil and cook to golden brown on both sides. Remove from skillet and place on paper plate to absorb excess oil. Continue frying in this fashion. Add more oil to skillet if needed to complete the frying.

FOR BAKING: To use less oil and avoid frying, spread a small quantity of oil on a cookie sheet. Place the breaded meat slices on the cookie sheet. Sprinkle a small portion of oil over each meat slice. Cover with aluminum foil and place in heated 350°F oven. Check after fifteen minutes. Turn over slices as bottoms brown and cook uncovered until fork tender. Depending on thickness of meat, some meat slices may take longer than others.

Note: I remember Mama making use of the remaining bread crumbs in the plate by adding them to any leftover beaten eggs. She then shaped the mixture into one or two bread patties. When I was a child, I stood at the stove watching with a watering mouth as she fried the cutlets and the bread patties. I waited for her to give me the bread treat to enjoy before supper. Today I smile quietly when I see one of my grandchildren standing beside me, waiting for that special treat before supper.

BROILED LAMB CHOPS

4 lamb chops
2 garlic cloves chopped or crushed
3 tablespoon olive oil
1 teaspoon oregano
1 large onion sliced (optional)
2 fresh tomatoes sliced (optional)
Chopped mushrooms (optional)
Salt and black pepper

In a bowl, mix chopped or crushed garlic with oil and oregano. Using pastry brush, spread the mixture onto both sides of each lamb chop. Marinate lamb chops in extra marinating mixture in a dish for at least thirty minutes.

TO BROIL: Lightly spray broiling tray with oil before placing chops on the tray. Place tray with chops in oven at least two inches under the broiling coils to broil fifteen to twenty minutes, depending on thickness of chops. Turn chops occasionally in order to cook on both sides. Broil chops until they reach the consistency desired. Before serving, brush extra marinating mixture over chops. Salt and pepper to taste.

OPTIONAL: Place tomato slices over marinated lamb chops in broiling tray. Then spread onion slices over tomato slices. Sprinkle a little oregano and oil over the onions. Chopped mushrooms can also be added. Cover broiling tray with aluminum foil before placing in the oven at least two inches under the broiling coils. Broil about twenty to thirty minutes depending on thickness of chops. Check for desired tenderness. Remove cover to allow browning. Salt and pepper to taste.

Serves two.

Note: I have grilled marinated lamb chops many times on our charcoal gas grill following this recipe. When I add tomato and onion slices, I arrange everything in a throwaway broiling tray, cover it with aluminum foil and cook over the grill. Then uncover them and brown slightly on the grill.

CABBAGE AND PORK CHOPS

4 pork chops
1 medium onion chopped
3 ripe plumb tomatoes or 8 oz. canned crushed tomatoes
2 dry bay leaf sprigs
2 small garlic cloves chopped (optional)
1 small head of cabbage
3 carrots
3 potatoes
1 cup of water
1/3 cup olive, canola or vegetable oil
Salt and pepper

In a twelve-inch saucepan, heat oil and carefully add pork chops. Brown chops lightly on both sides. Remove them from saucepan and set aside on a platter. Add chopped onion to the saucepan and simmer until onion is about to brown. Add bay leaves, garlic and cut-up or crushed tomatoes. Stir and cover. Simmer over low heat for about fifteen minutes.

Meanwhile, clean and wash carrots. Cut carrots into four-inch lengths and set aside. Peel potatoes and wash. Cut into wedges of one-inch thickness and set aside. Remove soiled or spoiled outer leaves of cabbage. Wash and cut into four or five portions. Set aside.

After tomato mixture has simmered for fifteen minutes, add one cup of water and stir. Add the chops and carrots. Cover and bring mixture to a slow boil. After ten minutes, add the cabbage. Ten minutes later add the potatoes. Additional water may be added if needed. Salt and pepper to taste. Cover and cook over medium/low heat until vegetables are tender.

Note: I remember that as soon as the cold weather replaced the warm days of summer, Mama changed her supper menu. The above is one of her winter meals. At times, she substituted frankfurters or Italian-style sausages for pork chops. During Lent she prepared a cabbage recipe without meat. She boiled rice for those who liked it and served it topped with the vegetables

EYE ROAST OF BEEF

4 pounds eye roast of beef
1 large onion chopped
2 chopped celery sticks
3 tablespoons olive, canola, or vegetable oil
1 beef bouillon
Aluminum foil or roasting bag
Salt

Heat oil in a skillet. Add chopped onion and celery. Simmer until onion is opaque. Remove onion and celery from skillet and place in a bowl. Add eye roast of beef to the skillet and sear all sides to retain juices in the meat. Cut a wide piece of aluminum foil in which to bake the roast. Place foil in roasting pan. Place seared roast in center of aluminum foil, or in a roasting bag. Gently add the oil from skillet. Place chopped onion and celery over the roast. Salt to taste. Cover roasting pan with aluminum foil to fully seal roast and contents (or place in a roasting bag). Bake in 350°F preheated oven for thirty minutes.

Meanwhile, add a beef bouillon to one cup of water and bring to a boil. Stir and turn off burner. Check roast after thirty minutes. Add a small amount of beef bouillon liquid and baste the roast. Cover and continue baking, basting every 15 minutes. Bake to tenderness of beef desired. (Approx. baking time—about 90 minutes)

Note: After baking this roast for my family, I place remaining bouillon liquid into a small saucepan over low heat. I stir a tablespoon of flour* into 1/4 cup of water and add to bouillon. Then I add liquids and onion and celery from the roasting pan. By stirring and *allowing all this to simmer slowly, contents will thicken into the gravy that I serve with the roast. *For thickening gravy, use approximately one tablespoon of flour to one cup of liquid.*

My family enjoys home-baked biscuits, mashed potatoes and salad with this meal.

MAMA'S LASAGNA IMBOTTITA

Baked Lasagna with Tomato Sauce

Lasagna:
1 1/2 pounds lasagna
Salt
6 cups prepared tomato sauce

Ricotta Cheese Filling:
3 eggs
One 2 pound container ricotta cheese
1/2 pound grated mozzarella cheese (optional)
1 tablespoon of parsley flakes
3/4 cups grated Romano or Parmesan cheese
Salt and pepper to taste

Place ricotta cheese into a strainer to remove any excess liquids. After ten minutes, place ricotta cheese in a bowl. Add beaten eggs. Use electric mixer only in very slow speed or stir by hand. Do not whip. (Optional) Stir in parsley and salt. Add three tablespoons of grated cheese of choice and (optional) mozzarella cheese. Mix thoroughly and set aside.

Partially cook lasagna following direction on the package. Boil lasagna only for five minutes or less (until the pasta becomes limp). Strain lasagna and return to pan. Add cold water to lasagna to avoid sticking together.

Spread some prepared tomato sauce over bottom of lasagna baking tray. Drain several portions of the pasta at a time from cool water. Avoid excess water in the baking tray. Place lasagna strips over tomato sauce in bottom of tray. With a tablespoon, spread ricotta mixture over the lasagna. Using a ladle, spread tomato sauce over the ricotta. Sprinkle grated cheese of choice over the tomato sauce. (Optional) Any meat in the sauce can be sliced and layered over the first layer of lasagna. Repeat the process until all lasagna has been layered into baking tray. Cover the tray with aluminum foil and set aside. Bake at least ninety minutes before serving time in a preheated 350°F oven for about forty minutes. Remove cover and check firmness of ricotta cheese by inserting a thin knife. If needed, return lasagna to oven until knife comes out clean and ricotta is firm. When thoroughly baked, set aside for at least thirty minutes before cutting into squares for serving.

Serve extra meat from sauce in a separate platter when serving the Lasagna Imbottiti.

Serves six.

Note: After the electric refrigerator replaced our wooden icebox in the kitchen, I recall that Mama often prepared her sauce and the Lasagne Imbottiti in the evening. She refrigerated the lasagna-filled tray and baked it the next morning.

Her favorite lasagna meat sauce was using ground beef and pork meat. She fried the ground meat loosely in her favorite saucepot. When the meat browned, she added the chopped onion and other ingredients accordingly to create her tomato sauce.

In the morning she baked the lasagna while she reheated her tomato sauce on the stove. A half-hour or so before serving time Mama cut her lasagna into serving portions. If needed, Mama retuned the lasagna tray to the oven at 250°F to reheat. I adopted Mama's way of preparing this meal because I found it more convenient than preparing everything in one morning.

MAMA'S RICOTTA GNOCCHI *(PASTA)*

3 cups unbleached flour (preferably King Arthur or Gold Medal)
1 beaten egg
1 teaspoon salt
1 pound ricotta whole milk cheese
4 quarts boiling salted water.

In a bowl mix ricotta cheese, beaten eggs and salt. Add flour gradually to the mixture, mixing by hand, until dough is soft. Remove dough from bowl and place dough on a floured pastry board to knead. If dough sticks to your fingers or hands, add a little flour and continue kneading until the dough is soft, smooth and pliable.

Cut and roll portions into long 8-or 10-inch rolls of about one-inch thickness. Place in bowl and cover. Taking one roll at the time, flatten roll *slightly* with your hand or a rolling pin. Cut into one-inch portions. With index and middle fingertips, press into each piece of dough and roll fingers forward in the dough. This will curl the dough into gnocchi. Continue until all dough is used.

For cooking gnocchi, boil about 4 quarts of salted water. After dropping gnocchi into the boiling water, stir and cover. Watch carefully because water boils over quickly. Gnocchi will float to the top as they cook. They cook rapidly. Check for consistency desired. Drain and place in a bowl. Add your tomato sauce and serve.

Serves four.

Note: I love the memories of watching my parents make homemade macaroni in our home. They didn't seem to have a written recipe. It was all stored in their minds. Through the years, I decided their recipes should be written out. I watched Mama measure out the flour, add the water or beaten eggs and all the necessary ingredients for gnocchi. Papa kneaded the dough. Mama always took out her extra-long wooden rolling pin when the dough had to be rolled into thin round portions before Papa could fold it and then cut it into linguine. For gnocchi, Papa cut up the dough after kneading it. Mama, with her fingers, patiently formed the small portions of cut-up dough into gnocchi. Before my brother Peter and I knew it, the homemade macaroni was ready to serve at noontime for Sunday dinner. They always made it seem that it was such a pleasure serving homemade macaroni, and it was.

MEATBALLS

1 pound ground beef or ground turkey
1/2 cup Italian-style bread crumbs
2 slightly beaten eggs
1 tablespoon grated Roman cheese
1/8 teaspoon of garlic powder or one small chopped garlic clove

Place ground beef or turkey, bread crumbs and slightly beaten eggs in a bowl. Mix ingredients thoroughly. Shape meatballs by taking a full tablespoon of mixture and rolling it in the palm of your hands into a ball shape. Place each meatball on a lightly greased baking tray. Bake in a preheated 350°F oven for about fifteen to twenty minutes.*

Remove from baking tray to separate meatballs from excess oil. Makes about twelve to fifteen meatballs, depending on the size preferred.

*To microwave: Place meatballs on a microwave-proof platter and cook for five minutes, then turn and continue cooking for five to eight more minutes.

Note: The aroma of frying meatballs filled the air in most North End apartments every Sunday morning. My brother and I waited for Mama to start frying her meatballs so that we could enjoy one before the noontime meal.

My recipe evolved from watching my mother prepare her bread crumbs for the meatballs. Most families had a special technique to acquire their desired taste. When I prepare my meatballs, I add one tablespoon of grated Romano cheese and one-eighth teaspoon of garlic powder (or one small chopped garlic clove) to the flavored bread crumbs. These additions give me the taste and aroma of the meatballs I remember enjoying in my childhood.

NONNA LUCY'S STUFFED CORNISH HENS

2 Cornish hens cut in half (4 pieces)
1 cup instant rice
1 medium onion chopped
2 celery sticks chopped
2 cups cubed (day-old) bread
1/4 cup pignoli (pine nuts)
2 tablespoons grated Romano cheese
1 tablespoon chopped parsley
1/2 teaspoon poultry seasoning
1 large beaten egg
1 egg white slightly beaten
3 tablespoons white wine
1 can chicken broth
3 tablespoons canola or vegetable oil
3 tablespoons butter or margarine
1 large garlic clove (optional)
1 tablespoon lemon juice
1/2 cup water

Cook one cup of instant rice in a saucepan as directed on the package. Cover and set aside.

Place oil, and butter or margarine in a skillet to heat. Slowly add chopped onion and celery. Stir and cook until onion is opaque. Add chicken broth and cubed bread. Stir until all bread is thoroughly softened. Remove from burner. Pour contents into a large bowl. Add cooked instant rice, pignoli, grated cheese, parsley, poultry seasoning and salt to taste. Mix thoroughly. Then add wine and stir. Refrigerate.

Wash Cornish hen halves and wipe with paper towel. Cut garlic clove in half. Rub garlic over skin of Cornish hens. Then rub a little margarine or butter over the skin. Spray roasting pan with vegetable oil. Place Cornish hen halves skin side down in roasting pan.

Remove stuffing from refrigerator. Add beaten egg and mix thoroughly. Cradle two to three tablespoons of stuffing on top of each Cornish hen half. Beat egg white lightly. With pastry brush, gently brush the egg white over the stuffing. This helps keep the stuffing in place. Cover and bake in 350°F preheated oven.

Mix lemon juice into water and set aside. After baking forty-five minutes, remove roasting pan from oven. Add lemon juice mixture to pan drippings and baste the Cornish hens. Continue baking and basting for approximately forty-five minutes or until Cornish hens are fork tender and stuffing has browned.

Note: At times, Mama surprised us with stuffed Cornish hens on New Year's Day as an alternate to roasted chicken or turkey. She often used a variation of her turkey stuffing to stuff them. My children and I continue to prepare this very popular meal.

NONNA LUCY'S TURKEY STUFFING

2 large onions chopped
3 celery stalks chopped
2 cans chicken broth
2 chicken bouillon cubes
1 pound of white or brown instant rice
2 tablespoons chopped parsley
1/2 teaspoon poultry seasoning
2 eggs slightly beaten
1 small French bread cubed
3/4 cup pignoli (pine nuts)
2 tablespoons grated Romano Cheese
1/4 cup white wine
4 tablespoons butter or margarine
Salt and pepper

One day earlier, cube bread and place in a paper bag to dry, or *slightly* toast cubed bread and cool on day of stuffing preparation.

Use one can of chicken broth as the liquid for cooking the instant rice and follow direction on package for cooking time. When cooked, cover and set aside.

Meanwhile melt butter or margarine in a large skillet. Add chopped onion and celery. Stir and cook until onion is opaque. Remove from burner. Carefully add remaining can of chicken broth to the skillet. Return to burner and heat broth slowly. Add cubed bread to the broth and mix until all bread is softened. If needed, add one chicken bouillon cube to one cup of boiling water. Dissolve bouillon cube and add gradually to bread as needed.

Combine rice and softened bread in a large bowl. Add parsley, poultry seasoning, grated cheese, wine, and pine nuts. Mix thoroughly. Salt to taste and store in refrigerator. When you are ready to bake the turkey, mix slightly beaten eggs thoroughly into the stuffing before you fill the turkey cavity. Place stuffed turkey into a proper-size baking pan and bake in preheated oven at 325°F until fork tender.

Since my family enjoys having some stuffing baked separately, I oil spray a 9" x 9" baking dish, or size needed to bake any remaining stuffing. Baste both turkey and the separate pan of stuffing with turkey pan drippings.

This recipe is for a fifteen-pound turkey.

Note: I remember the days, as a child, when I grated the cheese and chopped the onion and celery for my mother for her turkey stuffing. My children, who called their maternal grandmother "Nonna," learned to prepare this same recipe by helping as I had done. Now we have another generation—my grandchildren—eager to follow in this tradition.

NONNA MARY'S FRITTEDI

1 1/4 pounds ground beef
2 eggs
3 tablespoons grated Romano cheese
1 large chopped garlic
1/2 cup flavored bread crumbs
2 tablespoons olive, canola or vegetable oil
Salt

Combine ground beef, grated cheese, chopped garlic and bread crumbs in a bowl. Add slightly beaten eggs and mix thoroughly. To shape Frittedi, take about two tablespoons of prepared ground beef in your hands, roll and then flatten it to the shape and size of a hamburger. Continue shaping portions and set aside on a platter. This should make about eight Frittedi.

Heat oil in a skillet. Then carefully place Frittedi in the skillet to fry until thoroughly cooked and browned on both sides. To drain excess oil, place the cooked Frittedi on a paper plate for a few minutes. Then move them to the serving platter. The Frittedi can be cooked over charcoal or gas grill in place of a skillet.

Serve with your choice of vegetable or salad.

The remaining Frittedi can be added to a tomato sauce or stored in the refrigerator.

Note: My children called their paternal grandmother "Nonna Mary." This is one of her recipes the family enjoyed. She called them "Frittedi" because "fritta means fried" in Italian. She always fried them until they were well browned on each side.

I became familiar with them soon after my husband and I married in 1949. I recall her telling me that when her four boys were young and she had leftover Frittedi, she served each of them one between two slices of Italian bread for their noontime lunch. Some liked a slice of pickle with it while others added some mayonnaise. Though they are similar to meatballs, the garlic and extra grated cheese gives them added flavor when fried.

NONNA MARY'S LIVER AND ONION

1 pound calf's liver
1 large onion
3 tablespoons olive, canola or vegetable oil
3 tablespoons white or red wine
1/4 cup flour
Salt and pepper

On a cutting board, cut up liver into one-inch portions and place in a bowl. Sprinkle flour over the liver and stir so that all portions of liver are coated with flour. Sprinkle liver with salt and pepper and set aside.

Remove outer skin from onion. Cut onion in half lengthwise. Cut into 1/4-inch strips lengthwise. Set aside in a separate bowl.

Heat oil in skillet before placing liver into skillet. Stir to prevent sticking. Continue frying and stirring over medium heat until all portions of liver brown lightly. Add onion strips and stir thoroughly. Cover and fry over medium/low heat about five minutes. Check frequently to prevent sticking to skillet.

Meanwhile, in a cup, add three tablespoons of water to three tablespoons of wine of choice. When onion becomes opaque, add wine and water mixture to skillet. Stir thoroughly and cover. Allow contents to simmer slowly for a minute. Stir, cover and remove from burner.

Note: It always amazed me at how, in such a short time, my mother-in-law Mary prepared this Liver and Onions recipe.

"It's easy," she would say to me.

It took me a while to learn that liver does cook quickly in a hot skillet, then becomes brown over medium heat. Covering the liver portions with flour before adding to the skillet creates a delicious broth when the water and wine are added to the skillet.

Like my mother-in-law, I serve this with fresh Italian bread and a green salad.

POLLO SPEZZATO ALLA SICILIANA

Cut-up Chicken-Sicilian Style

A three-pound cut-up chicken
1/4 cup olive oil
1 large onion cut in quarters
5 cloves garlic
3 carrots—cut into two-inch pieces
2 medium potatoes–cut in quarters
1 large green pepper–cut lengthwise into two-inch wedges*
2 tablespoons wine or cider vinegar*
1 tablespoon dried oregano
1 fresh tomato chopped (optional)
1 cup green peas (canned or frozen)
1 cup mushrooms (optional)
1 cup water
Salt
*Two or three slices of prepared vinegar peppers can be used in place of fresh green pepper slices, wine and/or cider vinegar.

Heat oil in a saucepan and slightly brown chicken portions in the pan. Add onion and chopped garlic cloves to saucepan and simmer for a short time before adding chopped tomato (optional) and half a cup of water. Cover and continue simmering slowly until broth boils. Add carrots, potatoes, oregano and additional water. Cover and cook slowly for about fifteen minutes. Add prepared vinegar peppers or wine or cider vinegar. Stir and add mushrooms and peas. Stir and cook until chicken and vegetables are fork tender (about thirty to forty-five minutes, depending on size of chicken pieces). Salt to taste.

This recipe does not require a lot of broth but enough to serve some with the chicken and vegetables. Add additional water if needed.

Note: This recipe can also be prepared in a baking dish in the oven, or on a grill. Each method of preparation allows for a different flavor. When I prepare this, I remember when my maternal grandmother cooked this dish on our outdoor fireplace in Wilmington. I walked with her around the area, picking up small broken limbs and adding them to the fire. She told me that this made her feel like she was back in Salemi, Italy. During the harvesting days she accompanied her husband to "la mucarta" (a lot of land a distance from their home where they planted and harvested their vegetables for the year). At "la mucarta," she prepared their meals on the outdoor fireplace.

SPIZZATEDU

(Spiz-za-thay-doo)
Chicken in Bianco

1 three-or four-pound cut-up chicken
1 medium onion chopped
2 tablespoons chopped fresh or dried parsley
1/4 cup cooking oil
Grated Romano cheese
Water

Heat oil in a six-quart pot. Brown chicken portions on both sides. Do not burn. The browning of chicken parts in the oil and the browning residue remaining at the bottom of the pot gives the flavor to this recipe. Add chopped onion and parsley to the chicken in the pot after all chicken has been browned. Stir until onion is opaque. Remove from stove. Add enough water slowly to cover chicken contents. Cover pot and return to heat. Bring to a boil and then lower heat. Continue to cook slowly until chicken is tender. A chicken bouillon cube can be added if desired. Salt to taste.

Cook pasta of your choice according to directions on package. Place cooked pasta in a large serving bowl. Pour chicken broth over pasta and stir before serving. Sprinkle grated Romano cheese over each serving. Chicken can be served with pasta or separately, with fresh garden salad and garlic bread.

Serves four to six people.

NOTE; This is a recipe taught to me in 1949 by my mother-in-law, Mary Sinopoli. The family had migrated to this country in

1892. Her mother had taught her as a youngster how to prepare this "Spizzatedu" recipe that they had enjoyed in Messina, Sicily. It was a favorite of the family in the 1800s and continues to be so for the generations that have followed.

QUICK VEAL OR CHICKEN SPECIAL

1 pound cubed veal stew meat or chicken breast
1 large ripe tomato
1 medium chopped onion
2 cloves chopped garlic
2 small sprigs bay leaf (optional)
1 fresh mint leaf (optional)
1 or 2 *julienne potatoes
1 or 2 *julienne carrots (optional)
3/4 cup frozen or canned green peas
2 tablespoons red wine
1 chicken bouillon cube
3 tablespoons olive oil
1 can sliced mushrooms or mushrooms of choice
* (Julienne) cut into thin long strips

Heat oil in skillet and add cut-up veal or chicken breast. Stir and simmer to brown meat lightly. Remove only meat (or chicken) from skillet and set aside. Add cut-up onion and garlic to oil in skillet and simmer until onion is opaque. Add cut-up tomato. Stir and simmer over medium heat. Cover and continue to cook for two or three minutes. Then add to skillet one cup of water and a chicken bouillon. Stir, cover and continue to simmer slowly for another two minutes. Add cubed meat (or chicken) to tomato mixture and bring to a slow boil. Add bay leaf and mint (optional) to skillet and stir. Continue to cook at low heat for about ten minutes.

Meanwhile, peel and cut carrots and potatoes. Set aside in water in separate bowls.

When meat (or chicken) has cooked about ten minutes, add julienne carrots first. Cover and cook for about five minutes. Then add julienne potatoes and (optional) mushroom slices. Stir and cover. Continue to simmer until potatoes and carrots are fork tender. Add wine and cover. Bring to a slow boil and then remove from burner.

Serves two.

Note: Mama surprised us with meals like this at various times. I often wondered, now where did she find this recipe? *She loved creating meals that might be different. It was a great lesson for me. It encouraged me to create meals with meats, fish or vegetables that my family enjoyed. I suggest you try it, too.*

ROAST LEG OF LAMB

1 leg of lamb (5 to 6 pounds)
4 cloves of garlic
1 tablespoon thyme or oregano
1/2 cup chopped mint (optional)
1/4 cup lemon juice
Salt and pepper

Rub the leg of lamb with half of a garlic clove. Then make several gashes with point of knife into the lamb leg and insert small cut portions of garlic clove into the narrow openings. Rub meat with mint, thyme, or oregano, whichever you plan to use, or some of each. Rub leg of lamb with salt and pepper. Add a little water to the lemon juice and pour gently over lamb. Place lamb fat side up in roasting pan. Place in preheated 325°F oven uncovered. After 30 minutes, baste lamb with juices from the roasting pan and repeat frequently. Lamb should be baked until meat thermometer reads 175 to 180°F. If you are baking without a meat thermometer, allow lamb to bake approximately 30 minutes per pound of lamb. Add more water mixed with a little lemon juice if more liquid is needed for basting.

OPTIONAL: Small white potatoes, carrots and some mushrooms can be added around the leg of the lamb after the lamb leg has baked about an hour. Continue basting vegetables as well as the lamb.

Note: I awoke Easter morning to a combination of aromas filling the kitchen. I watched as Mama put the lamb roast into the oven. I saw the chicken soup simmering slowly on the stove next to the tomato sauce Mama had prepared earlier. I always asked to have one of the meatballs as she completed frying them. When did Mama start all this, I wondered.

On the kitchen table, a bowl of hard-boiled eggs greeted my eyes along with a Cannatone (Easter Bread) for Peter and me. As Peter, Papa and I departed for church after breakfast, Nonna and Mama's sister Lena arrived to help make the ravioli. I knew then that the Easter meal would keep us at the table for a long time.

ROAST TURKEY THIGHS ITALIAN STYLE

4 turkey thighs
4 medium potatoes
2 medium onions
2 fresh tomatoes
2 cloves garlic
1 chicken bullion cube
2 tablespoons olive oil
1/2 cup water
2 tablespoons lemon juice
Salt

Peel potatoes, garlic and onions. Cut each into quarters and set aside. Wash tomatoes and cut into quarters. Place washed and dried turkey thighs in a roasting pan (skin up). Distribute potato, garlic, and onion portions around the turkey thighs. Place cut-up tomatoes over the thighs, potato and onion portions. Add the bullion cube, lemon juice and water to the roasting pan. Spread the olive oil over the vegetables and turkey. Cover with aluminum foil and place in preheated 350°F oven. Check after forty-five minutes. Baste contents with liquid in the roasting pan. Salt to taste. Return to oven and bake an additional twenty minutes. A portion of water may be added if needed. Baste contents and return to oven uncovered. Allow cooking until fork tender and browned to your liking (approx. ten to twenty additional minutes).

*OPTIONAL: A*dd sliced green peppers or mushrooms to the recipe.

Note: For years, turkeys were available only during holidays like Thanksgiving and Christmas. Today the large bird is made available to consumers in cut-up portions. As an alternate for cut-up chicken, my husband and I enjoy turkey thighs. Turkey legs and/ or wings can be added to the thighs in the above recipe.

SAUSAGES, PEPPERS AND ONIONS

10 Italian sweet pork sausages
2 medium onions
1 large garlic clove (chopped)
2 green peppers
3 tablespoons olive, canola, or vegetable oil
2 tablespoons oregano (optional)
2 potatoes (optional)
Mushrooms (optional)
Salt

Place sausages in an 8" x 10" baking pan. If desired, sausages can be cut in half for baking.

Remove outer skins from onions. Cut each onion in half, lengthwise, and slice into 1/2 portions. Add to sausages in baking pan.

Remove stems and seeds from peppers. Wash thoroughly. Cut peppers lengthwise into one-inch portions. Add to baking pan. Sprinkle oregano (optional) and oil over ingredients in baking pan. Stir and salt to taste.

Other Options: Peel skins from potatoes and wash thoroughly. Cut up into two-inch portions and add to baking pan. Mushrooms can also be added. Cover and bake in preheated 350°F oven for thirty minutes. Check and stir ingredients. Cover and bake an additional fifteen minutes. Check, stir and return to oven. Removing cover for about ten minutes will help sausages and potato portions to brown to desired consistency. Serves four.

Note: This is a recipe that I remember Mama preparing many times at home. But when we had a large number of guests on a summer Sunday in Wilmington, Massachusetts, she placed her large blue porcelain baking pan with all these ingredients over the outdoor open fireplace. The aroma spread through the neighborhood as it baked slowly over the wood-burning fire. I remember thinking that baking it this way enhanced the flavor of this meal. Through the years, I have baked this on a charcoal grill as well as on our gas-burning grill. However, it needs to be checked and stirred often to prevent burning.

SCIUSCEDU

Shoo-shay-doo
Chicken Soup with Meatballs and Ricotta Cheese

1 three-pound cut-up chicken
1 medium fresh tomato (optional)
1 tablespoon parsley (optional)
1 medium onion
3 carrots cut up
2 stalks celery cut up
Salt
Acine di Pepe soup pasta
1 pound container ricotta cheese

For Meatballs: 1/2 pound ground beef
1/4 cup seasoned bread crumbs
1 slightly beaten egg

Boil cut-up chicken in a pot with sufficient water to cover the chicken. After water boils, skim residue off top of water before adding celery, medium onion, tomato (optional), some parsley and salt to taste. Bring to a boil and simmer slowly.

In a bowl, mix bread crumbs, one egg and ground beef thoroughly. Roll mixture into one-inch round meatballs. After chicken in broth has boiled about a half-hour, drop small meatballs, one by one, into simmering pot. Stir and cover. Cook slowly until chicken, vegetables and meatballs are tender.

About twenty minutes before serving, remove chicken from pot and set aside covered in a serving platter. With tablespoon, drop ricotta cheese gently onto top of broth, trying not to have ricotta cheese break apart. If pot boils too fast, the ricotta cheese may disappear into the broth. Simmer slowly only until ricotta cheese is heated (about five minutes).

Meanwhile, cook pasta as directed on the package. Serve with ladle into individual bowls. Add some soup, ricotta cheese, meatballs and vegetables to each bowl of pasta. Serve chicken separately.

OPTIONAL: Serve pasta with soup, meatballs and ricotta cheese. Serve the vegetables with the chicken.

Serves four to six.

Note: I learned about this recipe from my mother-in-law, Mary Sinopoli who cooked it for our family. She told me her mother always prepared this soup called "Sciuscedu" for Easter. The recipe came from her hometown, Messina, Sicily. Chicken soup has always been a popular meal for Italian families. I've often wondered why they called this "Sciuscedu." Perhaps the addition of ricotta cheese had something to do with the name.

TOMATO SAUCE WITH MEAT

"Macaroni with the Gravy"

1 twenty-eight-ounce can of crushed tomatoes
1 eight-ounce can of tomato paste
1 medium onion chopped
1 garlic clove chopped (optional)
1/3 cup vegetable, canola or olive oil
1 teaspoon dried basil, or 3 fresh basil leaves
1 or 2 pounds meat of your choice

Suggestion of meats and combinations:
 Ground beef or turkey for meatballs
 Meatballs and lamb stew meat
 Meatballs and veal stew meat
 Meatballs and Italian pork sausages
 Lamb stew or veal stew meat and Italian pork sausages
 Cut-up chicken portions

Heat oil in saucepan and brown meat in pot. After browning all portions, remove and set aside. Drain excess oil if desired, to limit the amount of oil in the sauce. Add chopped onion, garlic, and basil to saucepan. Simmer until onion is opaque. Garlic should not brown. Add crushed tomatoes and stir thoroughly. Add half a cup of water if mixture appears to be too thick. Cover and bring to a boil. Lower heat and simmer for about fifteen or twenty minutes. Stir occasionally to prevent mixture from sticking to the bottom of the saucepan. Then add tomato paste and stir thoroughly. Fill empty tomato paste can with water and stir water into sauce. Cover pot and simmer slowly over low heat for another twenty minutes. Then add browned meat. Cover and cook slowly until meat portions are tender.

Remaining sauce freezes well.

Note: During my years of experience in cooking, I have found that the taste of a tomato sauce varies with the kind of canned tomato used. My advice is to experiment with the variety of kinds of crushed tomatoes available today until you acquire the taste that pleases you. Try using a combination of meats in your sauce also, to vary or enhance its flavor.

Whenever I need a tomato sauce for preparing eggplant, veal or chicken cutlet parmigiana, I cook up a batch of this tomato sauce, **eliminating use of meat or tomato paste.**

VEAL AND CABBAGE STEW

1 1/2 pounds veal shoulder chop
1 small cabbage
1 medium onion chopped
3 small garlic cloves chopped
2 ripe tomatoes
4 small white potatoes
3 carrots
2 pieces dried bay leaf
4 whole cloves
1/4 cup canola, vegetable or olive oil
1/2 cup minute or regular rice (optional)
Salt

Heat oil slowly in saucepan before adding veal shoulder to sear on both sides. Remove meat from saucepan and set aside in a platter.

Add chopped onion and chopped garlic to saucepan and simmer until onion is opaque. Do not burn garlic. Add chopped fresh tomatoes or ten ounces canned crushed tomato. Stir, cover and simmer for about ten minutes.

Meanwhile, peel potatoes and carrots. If potatoes are large, cut into two-inch portions and set aside. Cut carrots into two-inch portions and set aside separately. Remove spoiled outer leaves of cabbage. Cut cabbage in half. Cover one-half with plastic wrap and store in refrigerator. Cut second half into three portions, wash and set aside.

Add veal to the saucepan. Cover and simmer about five minutes. Add carrots, bay leaf and whole cloves to the saucepan.

Stir, cover and simmer slowly about ten minutes. Then add potatoes to the mixture. Place cabbage portions over potatoes and carrots. Spoon the tomato mixture over cabbage. Add a little water if needed. Cover and simmer until meat and vegetables are fork tender. Salt to taste. Remove bay leaf before serving. Serves two.

OPTIONAL: Cook rice of choice according to directions on the package. Serve rice plain or with some tomato mixture over it. Then add a serving of meat and vegetables to the platter.

Note: I loved watching Mama create different recipes during the years. Now I encourage others, including my children, to be creative and vary meats and vegetables in recipes. For instance, this meal can be prepared using Italian pork sausages, or shoulder pork chops in place of veal shoulder. The meat used in preparing this will determine the flavor of the stew.

VEAL CACCIATORE

Veal Stew Meat or Veal Shoulder Arm Chop

1 pound veal meat
1/2 cup chopped celery
2 cloves garlic (optional)
1 medium onion chopped
2 large carrots
2 large potatoes
1 sprig of bay leaf (optional)
1 chicken bouillon cube
1 cup water
1 full tablespoon capers (in vinegar and water)
1/4 cup canola or vegetable oil
3 medium-size ripened tomatoes chopped
1/2 pound fresh string beans, or 8 oz. can of cut beans, or frozen cut beans.

Line a twelve-inch skillet with canola oil and heat over medium flame. Leave bone in if using shoulder chop but remove extra fat from veal shoulder chop. Place veal in heated skillet to sear and brown. Remove meat from skillet and set aside. Add celery, onions and capers to the skillet. Stir until onion is opaque. Do not brown onion. Add a little of the vinegar and water from the capers' bottle. Add bay leaf (optional) and simmer about two or three minutes before adding chopped tomato pieces. Stir occasionally and cover. Simmer slowly for about three minutes. Meanwhile, dissolve bouillon cube in warm water. Slowly stir in bouillon mixture into skillet. Add garlic and veal into skillet. Cover and cook about ten minutes over medium heat.

Peel and slice carrots into wedge about two inches long. Cut tips of string beans if using fresh beans and wash thoroughly. Peel potatoes and cut into two-inch wedges. Add carrots first to skillet. Cover and cook them about five minutes before adding string beans and potato pieces.

Add additional water if needed. Cook until potatoes and vegetables are tender. Season to taste. If bay leaf is used, remove before serving meal.

Note: I learned from my mother to vary the recipe by occasionally adding a can of mushrooms to the skillet. Another option is to add sliced green peppers or some green peas. In place of potatoes, I sometimes prepare some of my favorite rice and serve it plain or topped with a few tablespoons of sauce from the skillet.

VEAL KIDNEYS

1 or 1 1/2 pounds veal kidneys
3 cloves garlic chopped
2 small potatoes
1/3 cup olive vegetable or canola oil
3 tablespoons red or white cooking wine of choice (optional)
Salt and black pepper.

Remove any fat from the kidneys, wash and dry. Cut kidneys into one-inch portions and set aside.

Peel potatoes and cut into one-inch portions, wash and dry and set aside.

Heat oil in skillet to medium heat. Carefully add the cut-up kidney portions. There may be some splattering. Fry kidney portions until all are seared before adding the potato portions. Add chopped garlic and stir. Cover and fry over medium/low heat until potatoes and veal portions are fork tender. Stir occasionally.

OPTIONAL: Add the wine, stir thoroughly and cover. Simmer over low heat about thirty seconds. Add salt and pepper to taste. Remove from burner. Serves two.

Note: As a youngster, I remember Mama cleaning and boiling chicken feet to add to her homemade chicken soup. When I questioned the use of chicken feet, Mama told me that in her homeland it was customary to use as many parts of the slaughtered animal as possible—like chicken feet and livers, pig's feet, veal kidneys, and tripe. They had lived during difficult economical times. Ironically it prepared them for life in the United States during the

Great Depression. The meat markets of Boston's North End supplied them with all cuts of meats.

After I married my husband in 1949, my mother-in-law frequently prepared the above kidney recipe for us, knowing that it was a favorite of my husband. Today, veal kidneys are scarcely seen in supermarkets. Beef kidneys, more often available, can be prepared in this same manner. However, our family still prefers veal kidneys.

VEAL PARMIGIANA

TOMATO SAUCE:
1 twenty-eight-ounce can of crushed tomatoes
1 eight-ounce can of tomato paste
1 medium onion chopped
1 garlic clove chopped (optional)
1/3 cup vegetable, canola or olive oil
1 teaspoon dried basil, or 3 fresh basil leaves
1 pound mozzarella cheese (whole piece or shredded)
Grated Parmesan or Romano Cheese
Salt

Add chopped onion, garlic (optional), and basil to heated oil in saucepan. Simmer until onion is opaque. Garlic should not brown. Add crushed tomatoes and a half-cup of water. Stir thoroughly. Cover and bring to a boil. Lower heat and simmer for about fifteen or twenty minutes. Stir occasionally to prevent sticking to the bottom of saucepan. Add tomato paste and stir thoroughly. Fill empty tomato paste can with water. Add water to sauce and stir. Salt to taste. Cover pot. Simmer slowly over low heat for another thirty minutes. If desired, additional water can be added to thin sauce.

VEAL CUTLETS:
2 pounds thinly sliced veal (approx. ¼-inch thick slices)
2 cups flavored bread crumbs1 or 2 beaten eggs
1/2 cup of olive, canola or vegetable oil
3 paper plates or some white paper towels

Place prepared bread crumbs in a bowl. Beat eggs in a separate bowl. With a fork, dip a slice of veal into the beaten eggs. Place veal into bread crumbs to cover both sides of meat with the crumbs. Set aside in a separate plate. Continue in this fashion with each veal slice.

TO FRY: Heat 1/4 cup of oil in a skillet. Place breaded veal slices in heated oil and brown on both sides. Remove from skillet and place on a paper plate, which will absorb excess oil. Then place cutlets on a serving platter. Continue frying in this fashion. Add more oil to skillet if needed.

TO BAKE PARMIGIANA: Spread some tomato sauce over bottom of 8" x 10" baking dish. Add one layer of cooked veal cutlets to the baking dish. Cut up mozzarella cheese into 1/4 slices and place over each cutlet. If using shredded mozzarella cheese, sprinkle over each cutlet. With ladle, spread tomato sauce over mozzarella cheese. Sprinkle grated cheese of choice over tomato sauce. Cover and bake in preheated 350°F oven until the cheese melts (about eight to fifteen minutes). Use a spatula to serve the Veal Parmigiana. Top each serving with tomato sauce.

OPTIONAL: Include pasta of choice topped with tomato sauce to each serving. A vegetable salad and garlic bread go well with this.

Remaining sauce freezes well.

Note: Mama prepared Veal Parmigiana often when she expected visitors after dinner at our cottage in Wilmington. We ate dinner between twelve and one o'clock in the afternoon. On many occasions the afternoon visitors remained until suppertime. Mama felt comfortable having something extra prepared to serve for supper. She warmed up leftovers for those who desired them along with her Veal Parmigiana. Papa went into the his garden and picked some fresh lettuce while Mama selected a few ripened tomatoes and cucumbers to be added to the salad she served to everyone.

A VEGETABLE MEDLEY

2 medium potatoes
1/2 pounds fresh, frozen or canned string or cut beans
1 large garlic clove
1 medium zucchini sliced (1/2-inch pieces) not peeled
1 medium yellow squash sliced (1/2-inch pieces) not peeled
2 large ripe tomatoes or a four-ounce portion crushed tomatoes
1/3 cup olive oil
1 chopped medium onion
1 tablespoon capers
3/4 tablespoon basil
Salt

In a saucepan, sauté onion and capers in oil until opaque. Add chopped ripened tomatoes or four ounces of crushed tomato. If you prefer a heavier sauce, use a four-ounce can tomato sauce instead. Add fresh or dried basil. Stir, cover and simmer slowly. Meanwhile, peel and cube potatoes. Wash and set aside. If using fresh string beans, cut ends off, wash and set aside. Add potatoes and beans to saucepan. Stir, cover, and simmer slowly for ten minutes. Add sliced zucchini and yellow squash (optional). Salt to taste. Add water if more liquid is desired and bring to a boil. Cover and simmer *slowly* until all vegetables are tender. Serve with garlic bread.

Serves two.

Note: For those who enjoy rice or pasta, prepare your preferred rice or macaroni according to directions on the package. Serve a portion topped with the vegetable medley. Sprinkle with your grated cheese of choice.

AGLIA, OLIO, POMODORO, E BASILICO CON LINGUINE

(Aglia e Olio alla Salemitana)

5 large vine-ripened tomatoes (well ripened)
10 cloves of garlic
1/2 cup olive oil
1/3 cup fresh basil leaves
Grated cheese of choice
1 pound linguine
Salt and pepper

Cut up tomatoes into a thick medium-sized bowl. Add peeled and cut-up garlic gloves.

Wash fresh basil leaves. Cut up and add to tomato and garlic.

With a wooden mallet, crush contents of bowl into a pesto sauce (thoroughly mashed). Add oil, salt, and pepper to taste. Mix contents thoroughly. Cover and set aside.

Following directions on the package, cook one pound of linguine to your liking. (Reserve about one cup of water when draining the pasta.) After draining, place pasta in a serving bowl. If desired, add *a small amount* of the hot reserved water to the **uncooked** tomato mixture. Then spread mixture over the linguine. Stir and serve in bowls topped with grating cheese of choice.

Serves four.

Note: As I read this recipe, I can literally smell and taste this uncooked tomato, garlic, basil, and oil pesto. It became a traditional summer meal when relatives gathered on a warm August afternoon.

Papa always saved a few tomatoes from his garden in Wilmington for this purpose. Some of the children walked away from the table with teary eyes from the strong garlic flavor; but many grew to enjoy this special meal that originated in our parents' homeland of Salemi, Sicily.

Peter Orlando standing among the six rows of tomato plants growing in his Wilmington vegetable garden

ASPARAGUS OMELET

2 cups cut-up fresh, frozen or canned asparagus
4 beaten eggs or equal quantity of egg substitute
1 medium onion (optional)
1/4 cup olive, canola or vegetable oil
Salt

Cut up fresh asparagus, wash and par boil or steam in a saucepan. Set aside and dry with paper towel. To prevent dangerous oil splattering, be sure asparagus is dry before placing in skillet with oil.

Remove skin from onion. Cut onion in half, and cut each half into 1/4-inch long slices. Set aside

Heat oil in skillet before adding asparagus. Fry asparagus slowly for about five minutes, stirring frequently. Add onion to skillet (optional) and fry until onion is slightly browned. Stir frequently. Meantime beat eggs thoroughly in a bowl. Add salt to taste. Skillet should be well heated before gently pouring beaten eggs in a circular motion over the asparagus/onion mixture. Lower burner. Using spatula, lift mixture slightly. Tip skillet, allowing beaten eggs to slowly drain under the asparagus. Repeat this process on opposite side of skillet until only small portions of the eggs remain on top. Gently shake skillet over burner to keep mixture from sticking to bottom. Carefully slide the mixture onto a platter. Return the mixture face down into the skillet. Fry slowly until all of the eggs have cooked. Slide omelet carefully from skillet onto a platter for serving.

VARIATIONS: In place of asparagus, use cut-up green peppers, vinegar peppers, potato pieces, ham, or frankfurters.

Cheese of choice and/or mushrooms can be added to the omelet. Another option is to scramble all the ingredients in the skillet after adding the beaten eggs. Stir until beaten eggs cook thoroughly.

Note: Omelets or "Frittati," as my mother called them, were frequently prepared during my childhood. My favorite high school lunch was a pepper and egg (omelet) sandwich. Now that I realize what a strong aroma the pepper and egg omelet has as a sandwich I often wonder what my classmates thought when I opened my brown lunch bag.

EGGPLANT PARMIGIANA

1 medium-size eggplant
2 cups prepared bread crumbs
2 beaten eggs
8 ounces shredded mozzarella cheese
1/4 cup Romano or Parmesan grated cheese
1 cup canola oil for frying
Salt
8 ounces tomato sauce

Peel dark skin off eggplant with paring knife or potato peeler. Slice eggplant into one-quarter-inch rounds. Layer slices on a flat dish and salt lightly. Beads of liquid will appear on the slices as they rest one on top of the other. Cover eggplant with wax or plastic paper and place in the refrigerator for at least a half-hour. Meanwhile, warm up an eight-ounce can of prepared tomato sauce.

FOR FRYING: With paper towels, wipe beads of liquid from each eggplant slice before dipping into beaten egg. Then coat with bread crumbs and set aside in a platter. Heat 1/4 cup of oil in a skillet. Place slices in heated oil and fry until brown on both sides. Place slices on paper towels to absorb the oil. Then set aside on a clean platter. Because eggplant slices absorb oil as they fry, additional oil may be needed in the skillet.

FOR BAKING: Coat bottom of baking dish with some tomato sauce. Place one layer of eggplant slices over tomato sauce. Spread additional sauce over the eggplant, and sprinkle mozzarella cheese over sauce. Sprinkle some Romano or Parmesan cheese over the mozzarella (optional). Continue layering the eggplant in that manner. Then place the baking dish into the preheated 350°F oven to bake for twenty-five to thirty minutes. Check occasionally to see that the top layer does not burn. Remove from oven when cheese has melted. Can be served hot or cooled. Remaining Eggplant Parmigiana must be refrigerated.

Note: Eggplant Parmigiana can be served on a dinner plate together with linguine or spaghetti. This parmigiana became a favorite lunch in our home served to us between two slices of Papa's Italian sliced bread.

ELBOWS WITH ZUCCHINI

In Tomato Sauce

2 medium-size zucchini, washed and chopped (not peeled)
2 large ripe tomatoes or a four-ounce portion crushed tomatoes
1/3 cup olive oil
1 chopped medium onion
1 tablespoon capers (optional)
Basil and salt
1/2 pound elbow macaroni

In a saucepan, sauté onion and capers in oil until onion is opaque. Add chopped ripened tomatoes or four ounces of crushed tomato. If a heavier sauce is preferred, use a four-ounce-can prepared tomato sauce instead. Cover and simmer about seven minutes. Add chopped zucchini and dried or fresh basil. Add water if more liquid is desired. Bring to a boil. Cover and simmer *slowly* until zucchini is tender.

Cook pasta according to directions on the package. Pour zucchini with sauce over cooked elbows and serve.

Serves two.

Note: Spaghetti may be cooked and served with the zucchini in place of elbows.

LENTIL SOUP

4 cups lentils
4 cups of water
1 medium onion chopped
1 1/2 cups chopped carrots (optional)
1 1/2 cups diced celery (optional)
1 clove garlic (optional)*
2 tablespoons canola oil or olive oil
1 cup small shells or elbow macaroni

Wash lentils. Combine first five ingredients in a two-quart saucepan. Add chopped carrots and diced celery (optional). Bring to a boil. Cover and reduce heat to prevent boiling over. Stir frequently. Add more liquid as needed. Salt to taste. Oil is added just before lentils are fully cooked. Cooking time about 40 minutes.

*For a different flavor, add one clove of chopped garlic to lentils while cooking.

Follow directions on package to cook pasta of choice. Add lentils to cooked pasta and serve.

Lentil soup freezes well.

Serves two.

Note: My love for Lentil Soup came early in life. Whether Mama added carrots and onions or not, I waited for the Ditalini pasta to be served with the lentils. Sometimes, Mama preferred to serve the small elbow pasta with this soup. At times she served us the lentils with thin spaghetti that she cut up into one-inch pieces before cooking. Now I find myself also varying the pasta for this meal.

MUSTARD GREENS FRITTATA

(Omelet)

20 ounces frozen chopped mustard greens *
1 cup flavored bread crumbs
3 tablespoons grated Romano or preferred cheese
2 medium minced garlic cloves
1/2 cup canola, vegetable or olive oil
2 beaten eggs
Salt

Defrost chopped mustard greens in the microwave according to directions on the package or in a saucepan on your stove. Drain liquid and place mustard greens in a bowl. Add bread crumbs, cheese, minced garlic and two slightly beaten eggs. Salt to taste and mix thoroughly.

Add oil to a skillet and heat. Test a teaspoon of mixture in heated oil. When mixture sizzles, place the remaining mixture into the skillet. Oil should remain hot so that the mixture will brown but not burn. Add more oil as needed. With a spatula or fork, turn small portions at a time, careful not to burn. Continue frying and turning until the contents have mostly browned, about fifteen minutes. Then carefully slide contents onto a platter. Return the mixture face down into the skillet. Lower heat slightly and allow mixture to brown on that side. Then slide the contents back onto a serving platter. To remove excess oil, slide frittata carefully from platter onto two paper dishes. Repeat for the other side. Wipe oil from platter before returning frittata to a serving platter.

FOR FRESH MUSTARD GREENS: Clean, cut, and steam them. What is not used that day can be frozen in a container for the next frittata.

OPTIONAL: Because of the tartness of the mustard greens, try substituting ten ounces of chopped spinach for ten ounces of mustard greens, equaling the twenty ounces needed for this recipe. Try it both ways.

Note: My children request this frittata often but for them I use the combination of spinach and mustard greens.

My love for this vegetable frittata began when my parents grew mustard greens in their Wilmington, MA vegetable garden. Each summer, as Mama harvested them, she prepared this frittata for our lunch. I enjoyed my portion between two slices of Papa's scala bread.

NONNA MARY'S RICE AND PEAS

In Tomato Sauce

1 twenty-eight ounce can of crushed tomatoes
1 medium onion chopped
1 garlic clove chopped (optional)
1/3 cup vegetable, canola or olive oil
1 teaspoon dried basil
1 cup uncooked rice
1 cup frozen, fresh, or canned green peas

Heat oil in a saucepan. Add chopped onion, garlic, and basil. Simmer until onion is opaque. Garlic should not brown. Add crushed tomatoes and stir thoroughly. Add half a cup of water if mixture appears to be too thick. Cover and bring to a slow boil. Lower heat and simmer for about twenty to thirty minutes over medium/low heat. Check frequently.

Two cups of tomato sauce will be needed to cook one cup of uncooked rice. Set remaining tomato sauce aside.

In a separate saucepan, add rice to two cups of simmered sauce and stir. Cover and cook slowly for ten minutes. All the liquid will be absorbed in cooking the rice. Check frequently. Add more sauce or a little water to the rice if needed. Add frozen, fresh or canned peas. Stir and cover. Cook until rice and peas are tender to your liking.

If desired, top each serving with a tablespoon of the remaining heated sauce.

Serves two.

OPTIONAL: Precooked rice can be used in this recipe by

substituting tomato sauce for water in preparing the rice. Stir, cover and cook the length of time directed on the package. When using precooked rice, allow peas to cook in the tomato sauce for about ten minutes prior to adding the precooked rice. Remove from burner and set aside until ready to be heated and served.

Note: This is a meatless meal served frequently during the Depression. Enough was prepared for family members to have second helpings. Nonna Mary's favorite saying to our children was "Rice is nice." It always was when she prepared this recipe for the family, though our children sometimes balked about eating rice. She regularly had extra sauce available to add to her servings.

PASTA CON BROCCOLI

10 ounces cut-up broccoli–frozen or fresh
6 cups water
2 tablespoons olive, canola, or vegetable oil
2 tablespoon butter or margarine (optional)
1 cup cut-up spaghetti * or short pasta of choice
2 small minced garlic cloves (optional)
Salt

Break up spaghetti or thin spaghetti into two-inch portions. Bring six cups of water to a boil in a saucepan. Add cut-up broccoli to saucepan, cover and cook at a slow boil for about five minutes. Add cut-up spaghetti or pasta of choice to broccoli. Stir and cook until pasta is to your liking. *Add oil, butter or margarine. Bring to a slow boil before removing from burner.

*Variation: Place oil in a small bowl. Add two small minced garlic cloves to oil. Stir and add to broccoli/pasta mixture. Place saucepan on burner. Bring to a boil and then remove from burner. Salt to taste

Serves two.

Note: When Mama was needed in the bakery, she prepared this simple meal on a two-burner gas unit that Papa had installed in a back room of the bakery. Those evenings, we ate on a makeshift table created by turning over one of the 3" x 6" wooden bread boxes that my brother Peter or Papa placed on a few milk crates or wooden horses. We had family discussions during the meal just as we did in our apartment. Papa insisted on the family having meals together.

Meat did not have to be served for supper when Mama prepared pasta with broccoli because our family preferred having a second helping of pasta in place of meat.

PASTA E FAGIOLI

Pasta with Beans

1 can cannelini beans (white beans)
1 medium onion chopped
2 garlic cloves chopped (optional)
1 minced fresh tomato (optional)
4 tablespoons olive, canola, or vegetable oil
1 can chicken broth (optional)
1/2 pound pasta of choice
Salt
Grated cheese of choice (optional)

In a saucepan, heat oil over medium heat. Add chopped onion and simmer until onion is lightly browned. If using chopped garlic, add to onion. Stir and cook for a few seconds. Garlic should not brown. Add minced tomato (optional), stir, and cover. Simmer for about five minutes. Then add can of cannelini beans and stir. Cover cook over low heat for a few minutes. If sticking, add a little water or some chicken broth. Cover and simmer for about five minutes. Salt to taste. Remove from burner and set aside.

Cook pasta of choice according to directions on the package. After draining cooked pasta, place it in a large serving bowl. Add beans to the pasta and stir before serving in individual bowls.

Serves two.

Note: One of my favorite pasta with the beans is the small shell. However these healthy, hearty beans are delicious as well with Ditalini or elbows. I remember Mama sometimes cutting up spaghetti into one-or two-inch portions and cooking that for serving with the beans.

This is a meal frequently called "pasta e fasulli." It seems every Italian dialect has its own pronunciation for this wholesome and frequently prepared meal during the depression years.

SPINACH AND FAGIOLI

Spinach and Beans

1 can red kidney beans or
1 can cannelini beans (white beans)
1 pound spinach (fresh or frozen)
1 medium onion chopped
2 garlic cloves chopped (optional)
4 tablespoons olive, canola, or vegetable oil
1 can chicken broth (optional)
Salt

Fresh spinach: Clean and wash spinach. Set aside.

Frozen spinach: Remove wrapper from package, place spinach aside in a bowl.

In a saucepan, heat oil over medium heat. Add chopped onion and simmer until onion is **lightly** browned. Add chopped garlic and stir for a few seconds (optional). Garlic should not brown. Then add can of beans of choice, stir, and cover. Cook over low heat for a few minutes. If sticking, add a little water or some chicken broth. Stir and add washed fresh or frozen spinach. (Frozen spinach will require a little more water or chicken broth to defrost and cook with the beans). Let this simmer slowly, stirring occasionally until spinach is cooked. Add more water or chicken broth if needed.

Serve with fresh garlic bread and/or boiled rice of choice.

Serves two.

OPTIONAL: In place of spinach, use your favorite leafy vegetable of choice like escarole, chicory, mustard greens, broccoli rabbi or kale. *Note: I remember my maternal grandmother selecting her dry white beans from the various bean bins in the local grocery store. At home she washed the beans and started the long process of cooking them on her stove. The kitchen filled with the aroma of the simmering beans as Nonna faithfully checked and stirred the bean pot. In a separate saucepan she later used her cooked beans to prepare what she called "la minestra" (her beans and greens meal).*

During the Depression, mothers extended this recipe by adding more beans to the saucepan when needed. In most families, this often was a "dunk and eat lots of bread" meal because no meat was to be served that evening.

We are fortunate today to have various canned beans, which can limit the preparation time in preparing this meal.

SPLIT GREEN PEA SOUP

1 cup split green peas
1 medium onion chopped (optional)
1 quart of water
1 cup small elbow or shell macaroni
2 tablespoons of canola or olive oil
Salt

Ham pieces, ham hock, or ham bone are excellent additions to this recipe.

Wash split peas and place in water in a two-quart pan. Bring water to boil and add chopped onion, ham pieces, ham hock, or ham bone. Cook slowly, *partially covered*, to prevent overflow of liquids. Check frequently to prevent mixture from sticking or burning. When all split peas have dissolved, add oil and stir. Cover pot, shut burner, and move from burner.

Following directions on the pasta package, cook small elbow or small shell macaroni to tenderness desired. Mix pasta with pea soup and serve together with ham pieces or separately.

Pea soup can be frozen. Defrost first, before heating for use. Serves two.

Note: During the Depression, many of my relatives served Pea Soup often, as did my mother. This economical, nutritious, and easy-to-prepare meal was especially welcome on our supper table during the cold winter months.

STUFFED CABANELLE PEPPERS

Elongated Green Peppers

4 Cabanelle peppers (long light green peppers)
1/3 cup flavored bread crumbs
2 teaspoons capers in vinegar/water
Vegetable oil spray

With a paring knife, cut around the edge of the pepper stem to remove the stem and seed pod from each pepper. Wash peppers, dry outside of each and set aside. In a bowl, mix bread crumbs, capers and a little of the liquid from the bottle. With a paper towel, rub a little oil over skin of peppers. Place three teaspoons of breadcrumb mixture in each pepper. Peppers will not be completely filled. Spray a broiling tray with oil. Place peppers in center of tray. Turn your oven on to broil and place tray with peppers on the correct shelf for broiling. Peppers should be about two inches from heat. The outer skin of the pepper sears but should not burn, though a portion may blacken. **Keep checking and turning until all sides have been seared.** This only takes about fifteen to twenty minutes to complete. Remove from broiler oven, cover and set aside.

It is best to broil these peppers just before serving. If broiled in advance, they can be warmed up in the microwave oven.

These can be fried in a skillet with a little olive oil, but the flavor may be different.

Note: MaryAnn (Summa) Trodella, a childhood friend, treated my husband and me to these delicious peppers many years ago. She learned to prepare these from her mother-in-law who had immigrated to this country from Italy with her husband during the early nineteen hundreds.

ZUCCHINI WITH EGGS

In a Light Tomato Sauce

2 medium-size zucchini (not peeled)
2 large ripe tomatoes or a four-ounce portion crushed tomato
1/3 cup olive oil
1 chopped medium onion
1 teaspoon dried basil
Salt
2 or 4 eggs

In a saucepan, sauté onion in oil until opaque. Add cut-up ripened tomatoes or four ounces of crushed tomato. If a heavier sauce is preferred use a four-ounce can tomato sauce instead. Cover and simmer about eight to ten minutes.

Wash and cut zucchini lengthwise in half. Then cut each half lengthwise again. Slice each zucchini portion into to 1-inch pieces and set aside. Add chopped zucchini and some dried or fresh basil to the saucepan. Add water if more liquid is desired and bring to a boil. Stir and cover. Allow zucchini to simmer in tomato for about five minutes. Then crack eggs and gently drop each egg from its shell into the zucchini/tomato mixture. If possible try not to break up egg yolk once it is in the saucepan. Cover and simmer *slowly* until zucchini is tender and eggs are hard-boiled.

Serves two.

Note: This is a recipe prepared originally in our home with the elongated light green squash called "Cucuzza."

From the time I was twelve years old, my parents grew this vegetable each summer in their vegetable garden. The seeds, passed on to them by relatives and paesani, had originally come to this country from Sicily.

I have seldom seen this Cucuzza in produce counters of today. I know that it is still grown in home gardens by paesani (hometown friends of my parents) who dry and store some seeds after each summer's harvest.

Though zucchini is a great replacement in this recipe, I sometimes yearn for the sweet taste of the long cucuzza.

Lucy Orlando harvesting Sicilian long squash "cucuzza" from the Orlando Wilmington vegetable garden. Peter and Lucy shared the long Sicilian cucuzza with relatives.

ANTOINETTE'S PEANUT BUTTER BISCOTTI

DOUGH:
2 1/2 cups flour
3/4 cup butter
3/4 cup water
1/4 cup sugar
1/2 cup chopped walnuts
Two 6" x 9" cookie sheets

In a bowl cut butter into flour with a butter knife. Add sugar and then add water. Stir with fork until it looks like little balls. Do not knead. With you hands, make a ball of the mixture and refrigerate for one-half hour.

After one-half hour, cut dough into four parts. With rolling pin, roll each portion one at the time into a thin rectangular shape. Cover rectangular piece lightly with peanut butter. Then lightly spread jelly of choice over peanut butter. Sprinkle walnuts over jelly. Fold into a long roll beginning at side of rectangular piece of dough (about three inches wide). Place lengthwise (seal side down) in lightly greased cookie sheet. Continue to do the same with the remaining portions of dough, placing **two rolls** in each baking sheet. Brush tops of rolls lightly with milk for a golden color. Bake in a preheated 375°F oven for about twenty to thirty minutes.

For ease of handling, use a spatula to remove from baking sheet and allow to cool on cutting board. Cut diagonally into biscotti. Store cooled Peanut Butter Biscotti in a canister.

Note: I am pleased to share this unique recipe with you. A dear friend created it years ago. Antoinette (Marcantonio) Benda, sister of Dr. Joseph Marcantonio, and Rose Sinopoli decided to put together ingredients that she enjoyed with the hopes of making a different cookie. She created these delicate and tasty biscotti.

ALMOND-FLAVORED BUTTER COOKIES

3 eggs
1/2 cup sugar
2 sticks softened butter (1/2 pound)
3 cups flour
1 1/2 cups flour-separate
2 teaspoons baking powder
One or two cookie cutters

*1 teaspoon almond flavoring (optional)

ICING:
1/3 cup melted butter
1 box Confectioners sugar
"Jimmies" (sweet toppings) or nonpareils
*1/2 teaspoon almond flavoring (optional)

In a bowl, cream sugar and softened butter. Add beaten eggs and mix thoroughly. Measure out three cups flour and place in a separate bowl. Add baking powder to flour and stir. Gradually add this to the sugar, butter and egg batter. This will become soft dough. Spray two cookie sheets with vegetable or butter spray and set aside.

Spread some flour on a pastry board. Spoon a portion of pastry dough onto floured pastry board. Sprinkle some flour over dough. With your hand or rolling pin spread dough out to about 1/4 inch thickness. Before cutting each cookie, dip cookie cutter into flour. Then place cut out cookie onto greased baking sheet. Continue until all dough has been used. Bake in preheated 350°F oven. Baking time is about ten minutes. Bottoms will brown slightly. Remove from oven and place baked cookies on a tray to cool. Makes about four dozen.

ICING: Melt butter in top pot of a double boiler. Add almond flavoring. Gradually add confectioner's sugar to mixture until you have soft icing. Using a pastry brush, spread icing on one cookie at a time. Immediately sprinkle your choice of "Jimmies" or nonpareils over the icing. Set cookie aside on a tray. Continue icing in this manner.

*Use you own favorite flavoring in the cookie dough and icing.

Note: This is an easy recipe to prepare for a holiday or birthday party. The colorful cookies are a favorite of my children and grandchildren. They store well in a canister.

BISCOTTI

4 cups flour
4 beaten eggs
1 cup vegetable oil
1 1/2 cups sugar
4 teaspoons baking powder
3 teaspoons vanilla**
1 cup chopped walnuts *

Mix sugar and oil. Add beaten eggs and vanilla. Gradually add flour and baking powder. Fold in chopped walnuts last. Spoon mixture by tablespoon onto lightly greased cookie sheet, forming a long strip about two inches wide and one inch thick. Place each strip about two inches apart because mixture spreads while baking. Bake at 350°F in preheated oven about fifteen to twenty minutes or until firm with bottoms slightly browned.

Allow cooling only a minute. With spatula, carefully lift one strip at a time onto cutting board. With sharp serrated knife, slice each into 1-inch thick biscotti. As you slice, place sliced portions on the baking tray, side down. Return full tray into heated oven of 350°F for about ten to fifteen minutes to toast lightly.

After toasting, remove from cookie sheet to cool. These store well in a large canister.

**OPTIONAL: To make anise biscotti, replace vanilla flavoring with two teaspoons of anise. *Walnuts can be eliminated.*

Note: My sister-in-law, Rose Sinopoli, introduced me to this recipe around 1955. I have made them in my home ever since.

Rose began baking biscotti as a young girl. The family came to America around 1920. She learned to make these biscotti from her mother, Antonietta (Pisano) Marcantonio. These old-time popular Italian treats are wonderful with coffee, tea, or alone. They are also well received by family members or friends as a gift during holidays.

CANNALICCHI

"Kanna lee kee"
A Sicilian Christmas Fig Cookie

FILLING:
1 pound dried figs
1 cup red wine
1 cup water
1/8 teaspoon black ground pepper
1/2 cup fine chopped walnuts (optional)
Sprinkle of salt

DOUGH:
5 cups flour
3 tablespoons sugar
1 egg
1/2 cup vegetable oil
3/4 cup water

DAY 1: Place dried figs in bowl with wine and water to soak overnight. Cover and refrigerate. (Less liquid may be required if you are not using dried figs)

DAY 2: Chop figs or mince in food processor. Add black pepper, walnuts and mix in bowl.

DOUGH PREPARATION: Place flour, sugar and salt in a twelve-inch bowl. Add slightly beaten egg and oil. Add water gradually until mixture holds together. Remove from bowl. Knead to smooth consistency. Cut into four portions. Roll individual portions into long rolls one-inch thick. Cut these rolls into three-inch portions. Place in bowl. Keep covered. With rolling pin, roll each three-inch portion into long strips approximately 1 1/2-inch wide. Place filling in center of strip with teaspoon. Fold sides over. Turn so seam is on bottom. Press to flatten slightly. Cut pieces diagonally about 1 1/2-inch long. Longer pieces can be shaped as S's or U's, or round-like doughnuts. Slit sides with point of knife before baking. Place on greased cookie sheet and bake in preheated 400°F oven for twenty to twenty-five minutes. Tops will not color much. Bottoms will brown. Cool before storing in a canister.

Note: During Christmas week, relatives gathered in one of the homes to make this traditional Christmas cookie. I particularly loved watching my grandmother and Aunt Marianna shape thin rounds of dough with the rolling pin. Then they placed the fig mixture in the center of each round of dough and proceeded to gently pinch pleat the dough around the fig filling. It created a small tart. Not having mastered that procedure, I continue to shape my Cannalicchi as mentioned in the recipe.

CANNATONE

Easter Breads

5 large eggs
1/2 pound butter or margarine
6 cups flour
1 3/4 cups granulated sugar
4 1/4 teaspoons baking powder
3 teaspoons vanilla
Pinch of salt
1 beaten egg for egg wash
12 to 14 hard-boiled eggs

ICING:
1/4 cup water
1 1/2 cups confectioner's sugar.
Nonpareils

Cream sugar and butter. Add beaten eggs. Gradually add flour, baking powder, and pinch of salt. Add more flour if dough is too soft. Mixture should be soft enough to shape. Weigh out eight-ounce portions. Cut each portion into three pieces. Roll out into three long strips (approx. one-inch thick). Braid the three strips together and curve into horseshoe shape or circle. Nestle one boiled egg in bottom braid of horseshoe-shaped Cannatone. For round braid, place one boiled egg in center opening. Roll out two 1/4-inch-thick strips; long enough to crisscross over egg to secure egg in braid. Place bread in greased baking pan. Continue until all breads have been shaped. Preheat oven to 350°F. Makes 12—14 small breads.

Beat one egg. Brush egg wash on breads before baking. Bake at 350°F for approximately twenty minutes. Check after fifteen minutes.

ICING: In a double boiler, warm up 1/4 cup water. Turn off burner. Add confectionery sugar gradually to liquid until it is the right consistency to spread over baked breads. And sprinkle nonpareils before icing hardens.

To increase Cannatone recipe, add one egg and 1 1/2 cups flour.

Note: Mama boiled her eggs for the Easter Breads on Wednesday of Holy Week. She and Papa worked diligently on Holy Thursday to make and bake these Easter specialties of different sizes. They displayed them for sale in our bakery. My brother and I knew that Mama set aside a number of the smaller ones for the family.

At suppertime, anxious to eat one, Peter and I asked, "Which one is for me?" Invariably, she gave us one that evening. We hoped to have a second one for breakfast on Easter morning.

CANNOLI

Six to ten wooden or stainless steel Cannoli rollers will be needed.

CANNOLI SHELLS:
3 tablespoons shortening
3 tablespoons sugar
1/4 teaspoon salt
3 cups flour
2 teaspoons wine
2 tablespoons water
1 beaten egg
Canola oil for frying

FILLING:
1 2-pound container ricotta cheese
1 cup sugar
A pinch of cinnamon

SHELLS: Combine first four ingredients thoroughly. Add water, wine, and beaten egg. Knead dough into ball. Separate dough into small pieces (meatball size). Place in a bowl and cover. Roll each piece into a paper-thin round. Take one wooden or metal roller and gently wrap loosely around thin roller. To seal, dampen one edge of dough with a little water. It is best to prepare three or four cannoli before starting to fry.

FRYING: Heat oil in deep fryer or saucepan. Carefully slip the cannoli shell with roller into the deep fryer (or saucepan). With spatula or slotted spoon, turn item in oil to brown on all sides. *Use caution while removing hot cannoli from pan and from hot roller.* It is best to fry one at the time as they brown quickly. Cool thoroughly before storing in a covered container in a cool place. They remain fresh for two weeks. *FILLING SHELLS:* Drain ricotta cheese in a colander. Then place in a bowl. Add sugar and a pinch of cinnamon before mixing thoroughly by hand. Do not whip. With teaspoon, fill shells with ricotta cheese mixture. Sprinkle confectionery sugar over the cannoli shell before serving.

Note: It is best to fill the cannoli shells just before serving. Leftover-filled shells should be refrigerated. Filled shells will soften somewhat in the refrigerator.

CASSATTEDI

"ka-sa-ted-dee"
A Sicilian Christmas Ricotta Cheese Turnover

1 pound container ricotta cheese
2 cups flour
1 tablespoon orange rind
3/4 cups water
1 tablespoons red wine
1/4 cup shortening or margarine
1/2 teaspoon sugar
Pinch of salt
Pinch of cinnamon (optional)
2 cups cooking oil
Additional granulated sugar
10-inch Teflon skillet

Place ricotta cheese in a colander to drain.

Put flour in ten-inch bowl. Cut in shortening with knife and fork. Add sugar and salt. Mix while adding water slowly. Before using all water, work red wine into mixture. (Wine causes dough to bubble when fried). Continue mixing dough until it holds together and all flour is used. Knead dough to a smooth consistency. Separate into three portions. Roll each into a long piece. Cut roll into smaller portions approximately one-inch thick. Place in bowl and cover.

Transfer drained ricotta into bowl. Add orange rind, cinnamon and mix thoroughly by hand. With rolling pin, roll each piece of dough into paper-thin rounds. Place a tablespoon of ricotta in center of dough. Fold over (like turnovers). Press lightly around filling to allow inside air to escape. Then seal edges with crinkled pastry cutter or press edge with fork. Set aside on pastry cloth or a flour-dusted tablecloth. Makes about twenty-four Cassattedi.

Pour enough oil in a ten-inch Teflon skillet to cover bottom. Prick top of 6 Cassattedi at a time (with a pin) before placing in hot oil *top down*. When frying, turn each one with spatula until golden brown on both sides.

When any ricotta or fluid escapes into the hot oil, the liquid will splatter and burn. Remove Cassattedi from oil. Clean skillet. Add and heat new oil and continue frying remaining Cassattedi.

Place fried Cassattedi in a serving platter layered with granulated sugar. Sprinkle additional sugar on each one. Serve hot or cooled.

Leftover Cassattedi must be refrigerated.

Note: While I fry my Cassattedi each year with my daughter, my mind wanders back to the many times I stood with my cousins at Zia Marianna's black Glenwood stove on Charter Street. We waited patiently to sprinkle granulated sugar over our favorite Christmas treats. Then we served them to the relatives who gathered at the round kitchen table where we later enjoyed our Christmas Eve supper.

PIZZA GHENA

"Peeza Gay na"
Easter Ricotta Cheese Pie with Meats

CRUST:
1 cup lukewarm water
2 to 3 packages dry yeast
6 tablespoons vegetable oil
1 teaspoon salt
1 1/2 teaspoons sugar
1/8 teaspoon black ground pepper
6 to 7 cups flour – preferably King Arthur or Gold Medal
1 beaten egg for egg wash
1 9" x 12" x 3" baking pan

Pour water into a bowl. Sprinkle yeast over water. Stir until yeast dissolves. Add oil, sugar, salt, pepper and stir. Add flour gradually until all water is absorbed. Add additional flour if dough is too soft. Work dough into a soft ball. Knead dough for a minute and then separate into two portions. Spray vegetable oil lightly into a bowl before placing the two portions in it. Cover and let dough rise to twice its size.

Spray oil lightly over entire inside of baking pan. Moisten hands with oil for ease of spreading risen dough in baking pan. Then take one portion of crust dough out of bowl. Begin spreading and fattening it out by hand or with a rolling pin. Place it gently in the baking pan. Continue spreading by hand until the dough covers the entire inside of pan (including the four sides) **all in one piece.** Crust should be about 1/8 inch in thickness. Set aside.

FILLING:
8 beaten eggs
1 pound ricotta cheese
1 pound fresh formaggio cheese
1/2 cup freshly grated Romano cheese
1/2 pound sliced ham of choice*
1/2 pound sliced Prosciutto*
1 teaspoon salt
1/2 teaspoon black ground pepper

*Other dried cured meats can be added such as sopressata, pepperoni, and various salami slices if desired.

FILLING MIXTURE:
In a large bowl place ricotta cheese, fresh cut-up formaggio cheese, grated Romano cheese, salt, and pepper. Mix gently with a fork. Cut up ham and Prosciutto* slices into smaller portions and add to bowl. Add eight beaten eggs. Using a fork or spoon, mix thoroughly. Gently pour filling over bottom crust in the baking pan. Fill only about three-quarters of the baking pan, leaving about one inch or more from top edge of pan.

Spread top crust to about 1/8 of an inch in thickness and large enough to cover mixture as one piece in baking pan. Then place over mixture. With your fingers, gently crimp edges of the two crusts together and roll inward to seal mixture in baking pan. If desired, crimp edge portions with fork. This is necessary to prevent mixture from seeping through any openings while baking.

With pastry brush, spread egg wash over entire top crust. Prick three or four small openings of top crust to help moisture escape while baking.

Place baking pan in middle shelf of preheated 400°F oven for one-half hour. Then lower to 350°F and continue baking for about three-quarters of an hour. Then lower oven to 300°F and continue baking until the crust is golden brown. Check mixture after two hours of baking, insert a thin small knife into center. If knife blade comes out dry, mixture is cooked.

Cool this special Easter Pie for at least eight or nine hours for best results. Pie is served in square portions.

Makes sixteen to eighteen portions.

Note: Rose (Marcantonio) Sinopoli, my sister-in-law, has been encouraged yearly by her brother Dr. Joseph Marcantonio to prepare their mother's (AntoniettaPisano Marcantonio) original Pizza Ghena recipe. The family traveled from Avellino to America in the early 1920s, settling in Boston's North End before moving to Roslindale. For many years my husband and I have been privileged to taste some of Rose's delicious Pizza Ghena.

Because Rose makes such a large pie each year for all members of her family, she kindly reduced the original size of the recipe so I can share this smaller-size recipe with you.

REGINA

Sesame Seed Cookies

3 eggs
1/2 pound shortening (butter, margarine or butter-flavored Crisco)
1 cup sugar
3 cups flour
1 1/2 teaspoons vanilla
2 teaspoons baking powder
4 to 6 ounces sesame seeds
1 beaten egg for egg wash

Cream shortening and sugar. Add beaten eggs and vanilla. Gradually mix in flour and baking powder. This will be soft cookie dough. Place sesame seeds in a five-inch bowl. Using teaspoon, drop a spoonful of cookie mixture into the sesame bowl. Gently cover with seeds and place on lightly greased cookie sheet.

If desired, beat one egg. Using a pastry brush spread egg wash over cookies prior to baking. Bake in preheated 350°F oven for fifteen to twenty minutes or until done.

Makes about five dozen cookies. Store in a cookie canister.

Note: My introduction to the Regina cookies was in the 1950s when the family decided to bake and sell a selection of cookies in our bakery along with the Italian bread. This sesame seed cookie continues to be popular in my family. I prepare this downsized recipe to bake for use at home and to give as gifts during holiday.

RICOTTA CHEESE PIE

Cassatta

Recipe for one large or two 8-inch pies

FILLING:
1 2-pound container of ricotta cheese
1 1/2 cups sugar
3 slightly beaten egg whites (save yolks for piecrust)
1 teaspoon finely chopped citron (optional)
1/4 teaspoon vanilla (optional)
A sprinkle of cinnamon (optional)

CRUST:
3 cups flour
3/4 cup sugar
1/4 teaspoon salt
1 teaspoon baking powder
1/2 cup butter (or margarine)
3 slightly beaten egg yokes

　　Place flour in a bowl. Add sugar, salt and baking powder. Cut 1/2 cup of butter into flour until evenly distributed. Gradually add slightly beaten egg yokes. Mix to form piecrust. Some cold water may be added if needed to complete piecrust. Set aside a few minutes before rolling out piecrust (not too thin) and place in pie plate.
　　Place ricotta cheese, sugar, citron (optional), vanilla and cinnamon (optional) in a separate bowl. Add slightly beaten egg

whites and mix thoroughly until smooth. Do not whip. Gently pour ricotta cheese mixture over piecrust. Bake in preheated 400°F oven for ten minutes. Lower to 350°F. Bake until firm, approximately forty to forty-five minutes.

To dry any extra liquids in the pie, shut off oven and leave pie in oven with door open for fifteen extra minutes. Length of baking time may vary depending on liquid consistency of ricotta cheese.

Note: As a child, I sat on my perch (the wooden icebox) in the family bakery where I watched the bakers work. On Holy Saturday afternoon, when all the bread had been baked, I waited to watch Mama and Aunt Lena make two large 12-inch Ricotta Cheese Pies. After filling the pie shells, I watched them roll out l 1/4-inch strips of remaining piecrust and saw them create the lattice topping over each pie. It gave those pies such a festive look even before baking.

After placing the pies in the oven, they returned to the table to mix the dough for cannoli shells. My mouth watered in anticipation of the ricotta-filled cannoli I knew would be served on Sunday.

SFINGI

"sfeen-gee"
Fried Dough Christmas Treats

3 yeast packets (1/4 oz. each)
2 1/2 cups lukewarm water (105 to 115°F)
2/3 cup vegetable oil
3 1/2 cups flour
2 tablespoons sugar
1 teaspoon salt
A sprinkle of cinnamon (optional)

FOR FRYING:
1 quart vegetable oil
1 four-quart saucepan or deep fryer

In a ten-inch bowl, mix yeast with lukewarm water. Stir to dissolve yeast. Add oil. Gradually add flour, cinnamon (optional), and salt, blending all ingredients to form a *SOFT* dough. Cover and let rise to double its size.

Punch down and let rise again. Repeat two more times.

FRYING: Heat oil in small deep fryer or saucepan until hot. With teaspoon, drop portions of mixture into hot oil. They will fall to bottom and rise slowly. Remove with slotted spoon when golden brown all over. Place in large bowl. Sprinkle with granulated sugar. Serve hot or cooled.

Note: Though this delightful treat was also served in many homes for Easter, I remember especially waiting to see Mama mix her dough at Christmas time. Zio Nino and Zia Marianna's (Papa's uncle and aunt) top-floor apartment became a gathering place for relatives and friends on many holidays. What I remember most was seeing Zia Marianna, Mama and other women help to fry the Sfingi. The odor of frying dough was evident in the apartment and throughout the corridors of 39 Charter Street. My cousins and I served the hot, fried, sugared dough to guests arriving for supper. It became a special time after supper. The youngsters who had not fallen asleep after supper were welcomed to the round kitchen table again. We joined our parents in the games of Lotto (Bingo) with the other guests. A display of fruit, nuts, Cannalicchi, Cassattedi, Sfingi, or Strufoli remained available for all to enjoy until we departed for home.

STRUFOLI

A Fried Nugget-Shaped Pastry
Prepared for Easter and Christmas.

2 1/2 cups flour
1/4 cup sugar
1 teaspoon baking powder
1/2 teaspoon salt
2 tablespoons melted butter or margarine
1 large egg (beaten)
1/2 cup milk
1 teaspoon vanilla
1 eight-ounce jar honey
1 small jar nonpareils
4 cups cooking oil

Mix first four ingredients in a ten-inch bowl. Add melted butter or margarine, beaten egg, milk and vanilla. Mix to make dough that can be rolled into a ball. Cut dough into four or five portions and cover. Roll each portion into long strips of one-inch thickness. Cut strip into half-inch portions. Heat oil in small saucepan or small deep fryer. Carefully drop a few Strufoli into hot oil. Stir with slotted spoon. Cook until golden brown. Remove from oil with slotted spoon. Set aside in a clean bowl.

Heat honey in a double boiler. Drop Strufoli, a portion at a time, into warm honey. Stir a few seconds. Remove with slotted spoon. Place in a clean bowl. Sprinkle nonpareils over them. Continue until all Strufoli are coated with honey and nonpareils. Serve hot or cooled.

These do not need refrigeration.

Note: Mama made these for holidays because she knew that Peter and I loved to have some for breakfast with our milk or cocoa. She also prepared them for us to deliver a dishful to a few neighbors. She always reminded us to wish them a happy holiday.

I remember relatives and friends arriving at our home for a brief visit on Christmas and Easter morning. They brought us a bowl of their Strufoli or Sfinge. Mama or Papa also served the visitors a small glass of liqueur as they exchanged holiday greetings. Sometimes, Peter and I were allowed a small taste of the liqueur before savoring the guest's dessert.

Those precious moments always flash back in my mind when I am preparing my special holiday treats.